D1083863

The Rise of the Millennial Parents

Parenting Yesterday and Today

James M. Pedersen

ROWMAN & LITTLEFIELD EDUCATION
A division of
ROWMAN & LITTLEFIELD
Lanham • Boulder • New York • Toronto • Plymouth, UK

Published by Rowman & Littlefield Education
A division of Rowman & Littlefield
4501 Forbes Boulevard, Suite 200, Lanham, Maryland 20706
www.rowman.com

10 Thornbury Road, Plymouth PL6 7PP, United Kingdom

British Library Cataloguing in Publication Information Available

Library of Congress Cataloging-in-Publication Data

Pedersen, James, 1971-
The rise of the millennial parents : parenting yesterday and today / James Pedersen.
pages cm
Includes bibliographical references.
ISBN 978-1-4758-0536-9 (cloth : alk. paper) -- ISBN 978-1-4758-0538-3 (electronic)
1. Parenting--United States. 2. Parenting--United States--History. I. Title.
HQ755.9.P43 2013
306.8740973--dc23
2013035368

306.874
Ped

Printed in the United States of America

Contents

Acknowledgments

This book is dedicated to my two daughters, Emily and Veronica, and my wife, Faith. They are a constant inspiration to me and keep me focused on the most important thing in life: family. I would like to also thank my parents, Neil and Regina, as well as my step-parents, Dennis and Rosemary, for their continued guidance and support.

I would like to take the opportunity to acknowledge all of my former students, parents, and fellow educators who I have worked with over the last two decades. I have been very fortunate to have had many rewarding experiences and interacted with a great number of talented people. I appreciate my time as an educator and look forward to many more years of finding new and innovative ways to helping improve our educational system and help our children prepare for the future.

Preface

A LITTLE BACKGROUND INFORMATION

I am nearing my twentieth year in education and have found this time to be the most extremely interesting and truly rewarding experience in my life. In the last two decades, I have worked as a teacher's aide, a high school English teacher, a middle school tutor, a college professor, an assistant principal, and finally, a high school principal. These years have been countless experiences with students, parents, and community members that have all been rewarding. In full disclosure, there have been some great times but there have also been some very trying times, especially when you lose students to disease, violence, or other tragedies, where I doubted myself and wondered if I should continue.

Despite the frustrations that occur with teaching and being an administrator as well as the negative turn that the media has taken on the professions, I am still proud of my choice. I surround myself with dedicated professionals who know the vital role they play in helping prepare students for the future and who take this obligation very seriously. I believe that our profession is also unique in that each September is an exciting opportunity for new beginnings and new endeavors that are not afforded in other professions.

Teachers have always been expected to do more with less. In fact, resourcefulness is probably part of the very fiber of excellent educators. But never before, in my generation nor the generations that preceded mine, have educators experienced more of their students coming from such different backgrounds being raised in such different ways. This is not all a result, as some might think, of additional cultural immigration to America. In fact, many of the styles that will be outlined here are mostly uniquely American.

PARENT EXPERIENCES

Throughout the book I sometimes will make references to interactions with parents that I have had sometime during my career. The purposes of these anecdotes are used purely for illustrative purposes and in all cases I have sufficiently modified them so as to ensure total anonymity of the parents as well as my students, many of whom are adults themselves now, as well as parents of their own children.

It would be counterproductive, as well as downright foolish, to discuss the importance of building partnerships with parents and then go and expose some sensitive information that had been shared with me from my past. Parents expect teachers and administrators to be professionals who will keep their personal information confidential. Only under certain circumstances is information shared so that the teacher can better understand unique family dynamics and situations to develop strategies to address these issues.

I have had the experience of hearing some things from parents over the years that were deeply disturbing and extremely sad. Over the course of a career in education, a teacher or an administrator comes in contact with literally thousands of people including students, parents, siblings, relatives, and community members.

So, to all of my former students, parents, and colleagues, as well as my current ones for that matter, rest assured. All of the examples I have used in this book have been based on actual experiences from my time as an educator, but former students and parents will be hard pressed to find themselves in these pages. And that was entirely intentional.

In addition to my own experiences, I have also relied on discussion and conversations with other colleagues about the role of parenting in regards to today's educational climate. These professionals span from early childhood all the way to the college level. Although there are obvious differences in interacting with students from different grade levels, when it comes to parent-teacher relations, reoccurring themes always seem to surface. Although not the focus of this book, my college colleagues are experiencing more and more parental involvement than ever before. The colleges continue to hold their standards and continue to refuse releasing information concerning grades and other such things, but sometimes I think it will only be a matter of time before we may see a variation of parent conference night at the college level.

Introduction

The intent of this book is not to endorse one particular style of parenting as more effective or less effective than another one. Indeed, the idea behind the purpose of this book came from a genuine need and desire to gain a deeper understanding of the complexity of parenthood in today's culture. If, as educators, there is supposed to be a partnership between home and school, it would especially benefit teachers and other professionals to understand how diverse parenting has actually become. In addition to experiences from the classroom, resources such as news articles, blogs, Internet posts, research studies, and books from other professionals have been used in the writing of this book.

This book is designed to help parents and educators understand one another more and improve the communication between both groups. It has not been created for any specific grade level or age, but rather is written for a general audience so that all may benefit from it. Although each grade level poses some unique challenges, the information contained here is merely provided as a guide to provide insight into the many different parenting styles that are prevalent.

The idea for its writing was based on professional development workshops that stemmed from a series of conversations with educators regarding how much parents have changed in the last few decades. Over the course of the last twenty to thirty years, the entire parental landscape has undertaken a very dynamic change that isn't sufficiently addressed in the studies available today.

There may be an overwhelming urge to try and identify one's own parenting style, one's spouse's, or perhaps even one's own parents. Unfortunately, as many parents and educators realize, this is not as easy as one might think. But this is not the book's primary purpose. This catalog of approaches was culled to provide educators, and anyone else who is curious, the opportunity to view parents in an objective way to better understand them so that the students will benefit. The intent is not to alienate parents but rather to better understand the variety of different ways our students are raised and how these differences impact their performance in the classroom. The categories referenced here are meant to help identify some of the things already known and shed light on some you may not have known existed or have yet to experience.

This is not meant to necessarily be a straightforward how-to guide in how to successfully interact with every single type of parenting approach. It would be impossible to do so. As many teachers will be able to tell you, there are a myriad of factors that go into raising a child. In many cases, a teacher will not be even able to determine the type of parents of their students. In other cases, the style will be quite obvious. Hopefully, insight into the wide variety of parenting styles will help teachers raise their awareness levels to be more informed regarding what type of parenting is being used before the students even enter the classroom.

PARENTING TODAY

The new millennium has seen a variety of parenting styles that differ greatly from previous generations. Titles such as *tiger moms* and *helicopter parents* have received a great deal of attention by the general public but other styles, such as *hippo, free-range, divergent parenting*, and a host of others, are not so well known. These styles can be seen in public places, in television shows and movies, within our own families and especially in our classrooms across the nation.

Perhaps the greatest understatement one could make is saying that parenting is a difficult job.

In the twentieth century, experts began to provide recommendations for parents regarding the best practices for raising a child based on social, psychological, and behavioral research unlike the home-spun advice given to previous generations that pretty much amounted to *that's just the way we've always done things.*

But over the course of the last one hundred years, a variety of parenting styles, as well as deviations from the traditional roles that have been around for thousands of years, have emerged. Unlike these historical counterparts from yesteryear, who had to choose from the two to three popular parenting styles of their era, today's parents are bombarded with advice by everyone from certified trained child psychologists to anonymous bloggers on the Internet recommending what they feel are best parenting practices.

Parents and professionals are riddled with information that can be found on television talk shows, podcasts, Internet news, as well as a variety of other sources. It seems that what isn't lacking today are opinions nor ways they can be shared. Although information accessibility has improved, the discourse regarding best parenting practices and the inundation of information poses another challenge: sifting through the information to find out what is right for them.

It should be of no surprise that due to a number of contributing factors such as accessibility of information on the web and increased parent advocacy groups, the twenty-first century has become the age of choice and individuality. Unlike the past, parents today do not necessarily feel obligated to prescribe to any singular popular parenting style in raising children. The recent trend in parenting has become much more eclectic, befitting the diverse cultures and backgrounds of children of the millennium.

With such titles as *helicopter*, *submarine*, *curling*, and *fast food parenting*, and *tiger moms* and *panda dads*, parenting is on a much more diverse course. In fact, one would be hard-pressed to currently distinguish a dominant parenting style today as compared to previous generations.

Parents also no longer feel obligated to practice the same parenting methods of their own parents. In some cases, recent generations feel that if they follow their own parents' ways, they are most likely doing something wrong. For some, the old ways are the wrong ways and for others the old ways are the only ways.

Technology also has complicated the *art* of parenting. Not only is there information overload, but children are provided more visual stimuli than ever before. There is a whole generation of children now who experience the interface of an iPad tablet before printed paper.

WHAT IS A PARENTING STYLE?

There are all different types of parenting styles and a variety of ways of categorizing them.

Before the 1950s, parenting styles were rarely differentiated. Perhaps the broad categories of strict and lenient could be used as a general guide, but specific recommendations from "parenting experts" were practically nonexistent. There are many ways to define exactly what a parenting style is, but for the purposes of this book it will be defined as:

> *an approach that a parent or parents, knowingly or unknowingly, use in the day-to-day supervision and care of their child or children that incorporate one or more of the characteristics as outlined in one of the following categories:*

- *Hyper-parenting, hypo-parenting*

- *Traditional/neo-traditional parenting*
- *Millennial parenting*
- *Divergent parenting*

It is important that parents are able to articulate their particular parenting philosophy because it provides insight into the values they try to impart to their children and provides those children with the direction and focus necessary to grow and mature. It is equally important that as educators we stay abreast of current parenting trends because their impact undoubtedly will be felt within the classroom. There are some of my colleagues who will disagree with this stance, stating that too much has already been placed on the shoulders of educators in recent years and that understanding how our students are parented far exceeds our professional responsibilities; they would be right. Teachers have no place in parenting the students, but they must have an understanding of parenting styles in order to be better equipped to accept the challenges of the ever-changing landscape of educational expectations. Schools have increasingly assumed many responsibilities that were once relegated to parents such as nutrition, hygiene, sex education, and a host of others.

But why are there so many styles?

Perhaps no one is really able to provide a satisfactory answer to this but as the nation becomes more diverse, there is a need for individual expression that reflects the diversity that is occurring in the American population. Another reason would most likely have to do with the blending of so many cultures that creates mixtures which may have not been present in the nation before.

Family structures are also much more diverse than in previous generations. For example, never before in the history of the United States do we have such a variety in the different types of families that exist in our country. Examine just a few of the many types of combinations that currently exist:

- Two-parent households where both parents work and the children are cared for by before-care, school, and after-care programs
- Two-parent households where one parent goes out to work and the other stays home to care for the children
- Two-parent households where both parents go out to work and another family member, like a grandparent or an aunt, cares for the children
- Single-parent households where children are cared for by before-care, school, and after- care programs
- Single-parent households where the parent is unemployed or disabled and cares for the children

To further complicate matters, today's generation of children may be raised in a variety of different home environments:

- Two heterosexual parents
- Two parents from the gay, bisexual, lesbian or transgender community (GBLT)
- Single heterosexual parent
- Single GBLT parent
- Foster parents
- Children raised by other family members

As most professionals already know, the categories of parents are not as important as the individual or individuals who assume the parenting roles. The purpose for using these categories here, as well as in other places in this book, is to illustrate the vast range of combinations that represent the families of students in the American school system.

This book has been organized so that the reader will have a basic overview of the myriad of parenting factors that examine the socioeconomic influences as well as the interactions between other factors. The following sections are presented in a way that provides a brief overview of each category with specific styles. Each style is given explanations with possible motivations and how teachers can best interact with these specific parenting styles.

Lastly, in most recent times, the economy is perhaps one of the most important driving forces that influence how children are being raised today. Financial constraints have forced many parents to work longer hours and make additional sacrifices that most often result in spending less time at home with their families and raising their children. Therefore, the little quality time that is left for families to spend together is devoted to "catching up" on the things they have been missing. Often, parents do not like spending what little time they have disciplining their children, which is a crucial part of parenting.

Chapter One

Parenting Factors

SOCIOECONOMIC DIFFERENCES

Annette Lareau, a sociologist at the University of Pennsylvania, completed a study of child-rearing practices of African-American and European-American families that focused on financial and cultural influences on American families (2011). Not surprisingly, her results found that the amount of money that a family has influences the type of parenting styles they employ and can even preclude others. For example, it is very difficult for a single working mother to be able to try *slow parenting* due to exhaustive work schedules and financial constraints. Parents from low socioeconomic levels might not even have the resources to seek other types of parenting styles other than those that already exist in their community, whereas their higher socioeconomic counterparts have more resources available to them.

As is most often the case, money is always an issue and raising a family is no exception. More money does not always mean that parenting becomes easier, but it does provide opportunities for more time together as well as additional resources that could not be provided from other socioeconomic groups.

But the difference with this issue is that more money does not necessarily mean better parenting. In fact, in some cases it can make matters even worse. Children of two working parents may have problems, although different, just like the child of two low-income unemployed parents on public assistance. It is really the motivation of the parents to consciously adopt, or subconsciously adopt in some other cases, an approach that works best for them in raising their children.

THE INTERACTION OF TWO PARENTING STYLES

Although it does happen on occasion, I have very seldom encountered both parents who share the exact same approach to raising their children. When it does occur, it is like a beautiful harmony, but when it doesn't it can be quite horrendous. In some cases, they can be similar styles but one tends to be committed to the approach while the other assists in the maintenance of the style of the other parent.

Most often I find that when the styles do differ that then the approaches can complement each other. For example, two *hypoparenting* styles tend to work together productively whereas a *divergent* and a *hypoparent* would most definitely clash. In addition, the *traditional/neo-traditional* styles and the *millennial* styles will most often work with other styles to some degree. These conflicts can cause many problems for the family, affecting how children will develop and mature.

Conflicting parenting styles can pose some serious challenges for teachers in the classroom as well. For example, a *helicopter* and a *free-range* parent are going to have some major conflicts regarding how best to raise their children. When these conflicts occur, it is always advisable that teachers make sure not to get between the two parents in their parenting. Keeping conversations focused on classroom behaviors and expectations will always be more productive. I have had the unfortunate experience of being caught between conflicting parenting styles in my career, and these situations have always made me feel uneasy. Some parents seek validation of their style and will view the teacher as professional who can be used as an ally to prove the other parent wrong. These situations happen often in situations where there is divorce or separation but could just as easily occur in intact relationships as well.

Teachers will be caught in the middle of family issues when one parent requests one way to handle a situation while the other parent has an entirely different way of addressing it. In these cases, teachers can find themselves in a tug of war regarding discipline issues and classroom expectations.

The first step to addressing these situations is to always make sure that student records are current and up to date. It is always detrimental to find out that a parent you have conversed with all year no longer has custodial rights because no one from the guidance department had informed you. The next thing is to make sure that the ground rules for parent-teacher conferences are clearly established. Stick to the prearranged topic and make sure that everyone leaves with the same action plan in clearly explained objectives.

PARENTAL INFLUENCE IN THE CLASSROOM

There will be many parents who clearly articulate what type of parenting style they use and will communicate this with their children's teachers. They usually do this because they want to let the teacher know how their child is raised at home with the expectations that the teacher can either reinforce those attributes in school or at the very least not undermine the rules they have set in place.

Other parents, on the other hand, will not be as clear with their expectations with teachers. Some professionals may even prefer not to place an emphasis on knowing how a child is raised because it should have little effect on what occurs in the class. For the most part, this is true and I agree. What occurs at the home should not impact instruction, but the reality is that over the last few decades I have witnessed a sharp decrease in the autonomy and control teachers and administrators once had in the schools replaced with more parental scrutiny than ever before. I wonder if parents, who view themselves as consumers, operate on our current consumer model where customers are more informed and more demanding. After all, we exist in a time where customers are free to leave public feedback on how they feel about a purchased product.

Alas, the days of the "teacher is always right" have all but faded. Parents are not as willing to accept what educators say at face value and now have the resources to make better informed decisions about their children's education. This, of course, poses new challenges as the parent-teacher dynamic is continuously morphing into a different type of partnership.

For example, because of technological advancements, parents are now afforded more opportunity than ever before to find out how their children are performing in school. Online grade books, once a novelty, are nearly almost a requirement in most schools. And for every parent who never checks their child's academic status, it seems that there are least two who check it regularly and expect it to be updated on an immediate basis. When one considers the amount of information that is currently available to parents today, it is quite astounding. Resources such as:

- Online grades
- Schedules
- Teacher contact numbers and email
- Board agenda minutes
- Curriculum guides
- Parent and student handbooks
- Calendars
- School report cards
- State and national standards

- A whole host of other things with more to come in the future

It's no wonder why parents expect so much more—because the consumer expects so much more as well.

Parent conferences may have decreased over the years, but the frequency of communication, whether it is voicemail, email, or texts, has greatly increased. Parents now can send an email at eleven o'clock at night with a question about an assignment and expect a response within a reasonable amount of time. In some of the younger grades, teachers are expected to keep the parents current with classroom activities through electronic newsletters, websites, or blogs.

Lastly, having spent nearly two decades at the secondary level, I have noticed how parents of high school students have exhibited many of the characteristics of involvement once found only at the elementary and middle school levels. I have received many more phone calls in recent years from parents exhibiting enabling behaviors to get their children excused from projects, lateness, or other disciplinary infractions as compared to earlier in my career when expectations for high school students were placed on the adolescents themselves.

I am always careful about these kinds of statements because I prefer not to be lumped into individuals who begin every sentence with, "Kids today …" or "When I was a kid …" for two reasons. For one reason, it is too cliché and for the other, it just sounds too much like a cop-out. Adults always have a way of looking back and romanticizing or dramatizing their past depending on their intent.

I think that the reason parents of high school students are exhibiting characteristics that were once considered elementary school types of involvement simply can be attributed to increased life expectancies and academic inflation. As people live longer in this country, they have been given longer time to mature (Do you remember when kids moved out and on their own when they were eighteen?) and are being urged to attend some postsecondary institution to keep up with the job market (Do you remember when a college diploma in any area was good enough?).

All of these things lead to increased and intense parental involvement that looks very different from previous generations and encourages parents and teachers to know a little bit more about each other.

In the past, I have given my staff the analogy of how one goes about purchasing a car has changed in recent decades. When I bought my first new car, I was left to rely on the little information that was available to me at the time.

I first talked to the salesperson. I then went home and talked to family members who had experience with buying cars. I then asked some friends who knew about cars and eventually went back and asked the salesperson additional questions. This entire process took several days to a week before I felt that I had enough information to purchase the vehicle. Some of my friends took an easier approach of just buying from the same manufacturer that their fathers had used.

Once upon a time there was a thing call brand loyalty.

That isn't true today: the ordeal of buying a car nor brand loyalty. Most people don't go the showroom until they are finished doing their research and comparing products. When they arrive at the dealership, they are ready to discuss price, on which they also have done their research. They are able to find competitor prices, user reviews, and entire websites dedicated to how to purchase a new vehicle.

After sharing this analogy, I asked my staff if they thought that there are some parents out there doing the same thing. Nowhere is this more evident than with parents of children who receive special services. Over the years, these parents have become much more informed and aware of their rights and accommodations. In addition to the information that is available on the Internet, they have also started blogs and user groups to share valuable information.

So, if the parents are more aware of all the information that schools have to offer, it would behoove educators to understand the variety of ways parents are choosing to raise their children.

I was once asked why the number of various parenting styles is so surprising to many educators. One would think that they are well aware of the children coming into their classroom. The truth is that I think teachers, only if it became a problem, would even venture to think how the children were being raised.

As a matter of fact, many veteran educators would say that although there are always exceptions, the way a child was raised mattered very little to how they were expected to act while they were with them in the classroom. Today that seems to be less of a case. The way children are being raised has more of an effect on what is happening in the classroom than ever before.

This is not to mean that teachers should dictate a particular style nor should they be expected to conduct parenting class. Indeed, the responsibilities of teachers are already far too great and numerous. High stakes testing, intervention, national standards, mental health, and a variety of other responsibilities are already enough for them to handle.

I think that teachers should use this information to increase their awareness to understand how complicated life has become; knowing the many varieties of parenting might help teachers to ease some of their frustration with why things that may have worked in the past might not be as effective in the present and the future.

In the business of education, our clients have changed and they are expecting more than ever before.

DIFFERENCES IN AGE

Differences in the ages of the parents may also play an influential role in the type of parenting style that is ultimately used within the family. For example, the styles young parents might adopt can be different from parents who are older. Life experiences, maturity, and a host of other factors can play into the various styles parents choose to adopt.

Although, as I have been proven many times, age does not always ensure wisdom, there is a general feeling that many younger parents are more inclined to seek parenting advice from other sources such as books and classes. Older parents, on the other hand, may use more traditional/neo-traditional methods of child rearing. Of course, I have found the opposite to be true in many cases as well.

In my experience, age only really begins to pose challenges to teachers when parents are at the two extremes: very young or very … not young.

It is in these two groups that I have found some challenge may exist. For example, I have found more *best friend*, *pussy cat*, and *detached parents* from a younger parenting demographic than I would from their older counterparts. Likewise, I have found more *hot-tub* and *slow parenting* from older parents who view the world differently from their younger peers.

PARENTING STYLES AND MULTIPLE CHILDREN

In some cases, the number of children in a family can also impact how parents decide to raise their children. The number of children and the age differences amongst them can also play a role in which approach parents use and if they even decide to remain consistent with their parenting style with all of their children. In some cases parents may use the same approach with all of their children regardless of how many they have, while in other instances they may vary their style with each individual child.

Let's first look at children who do not have any siblings. During my experience in the public school system, an overwhelming majority of the *hyper-parenting* parents tend to have only one child. These parents generally seem to exhibit characteristics that one would most often expect from a family where one child receives all of the attention in the family.

Children from families with one or more siblings can be different, however.

Research by Alfred Adler (1937) highlighted the importance of birth order and how it can impact personality traits. First-born siblings have been found to take on leadership roles and are usually described as reliable or dependable, whereas the youngest sibling may take on attributes such as self-centeredness and insecurity. These characteristics are often attributed to birth order, but how the parents approach raising each child may be of equal or even greater importance. And what I find most interesting is how the parenting styles might change with each child and how those styles can affect student behavior in the classroom.

For example, a parent might adopt a *hyper-parenting* style with the first-born child and become more *traditional/neo-traditional* or even *hypo-parenting* with each successive child.

In addition to their birth order, children may also exhibit their own characteristics that would motivate their parents to raise them in a certain fashion more suited to their individual personalities.

HOW SEX AFFECTS PARENTING

The sex of the children, as well as the parents, may also contribute to the influence of adopting certain parenting styles.

For example, the sex of the parent may in certain circumstances play a significant role in what type of parenting style is used. Although traditionally in the past male parents have often been designated as the disciplinarians, today's families can look quite different. Due to the variety of family structures already covered, previous traditional gender roles may not apply in all circumstances as they once were.

The sex of the child is also sometimes important in determining how a parent will raise the child. For many reasons, girls may be raised with much more scrutiny than their male counterparts. Certain *hyper-parenting* styles lend themselves to traditional stereotypes regarding the needs for boy and girls, but *millennial* parenting also provides for the adoption of new paradigms as well.

SITUATIONAL PARENTING STYLES

Although parents may prescribe to a particular approach, various situations may occur in their lives that would cause them to deviate to adopt characteristics from other styles in order to accomplish their specific goals. For example, I recall one *commando parent* who never tolerated any bad behavior from her child practically transform into a *volcano parent* when her daughter was caught in a serious situation that involved her being found with illegal drugs in her possession. The penalties that she faced were quite severe and the mother, who had never before made any excuses for her daughter, began to make excuse after excuse to prevent her daughter from those legal ramifications.

I have noticed other style shifts for other reasons such as:

- Death of another child
- Change in occupation
- Economic factors
- Divorce or separation
- Any other change in the family dynamic

HOW PARENTING STYLES IMPACT THE EDUCATIONAL SETTING

The teacher-parent relationship has been compared to a lot of different things: a business partnership, an adversarial relationship, and even an arranged marriage (Mosle, 2013). The reality is that it can be all of those things—and a whole lot more. At its best, it is a great relationship characterized by mutual respect and understanding with both parties participating in a collaborative effort to tend to the academic and emotional needs of the child. At its most challenging, it can be a stressful and potentially dangerous arena where distrust, animosity, and vitriol are present at every turn as the focus on the student is lost as one or both sides force their agendas, believing their view is the only means of addressing the student's needs.

And this is where understanding is needed from both parties, but as professionals the burden of this responsibility usually winds up on teachers' backs. For the most part, teachers may not even know the parenting styles of many of their students because it isn't necessary knowledge and doesn't impact the classroom. But as in most situations, *a problem isn't a problem until it becomes a problem.*

Although a little repetitive, this advice has become a mantra for me in my professional life.

As a matter of fact, when I was a teacher and minor student issues rose, I very seldom thought about how parenting affected the student's behavior. It was only when persistent problems or issues reoccurred that I even thought of how parenting helped or worsened the situation in the classroom.

The information that follows is important for all parents and professionals but even more so for educators who need to stay current with the latest parenting trends because each approach has reverberating effects in the classroom. Due to the constantly expanding parenting choices that this current generation is producing, the rest of this book attempts to identify some of the more popular styles that currently exist and should be used as a starting point for further discussions, but it is in no way meant to be comprehensive.

PARENT PROFILING

Based on the information provided so far, it may seem that I am interested in *parent profiling.*

I am not.

I decided to share the information in this book partly because I believe that there are many educators and parents out there who naturally put things in categories to better understand them. I am sure part of this is some sort of control issue that lies within my subconscious, but I believe that the real impetus is based on my sincere desire to better understand people.

I have tried my best to keep as much subjectivity as possible from these pages, but I'm sure some will still find its way to the surface; that has never been my intent. I feel that chronicling the wide expanse of parenting practices that exist in our nation allows educators to better serve the students in their classrooms because it prepares us for challenges that can present themselves.

Chapter Two

Parenting in the Twentieth Century

The early twentieth century saw a significant difference in parenting by moving from the traditionally based child rearing to the modern approach of child rearing. Parents during this modern time became much more interested in and aware of child development through education and early training (Lynd, 1929). Prior to twentieth century, however, children were often viewed as little adults whose responsibilities to the family were more pressing than the need for childhood development.

For the vast majority, children in those days were merely a form of cheap labor that helped to support the family until they reached an age where they would get married and start families of their own. Only wealthy families had the luxury and privilege of sending their children to school, allowing them to escape the child labor practices. By the late 1920s, however, psychologist Sigmund Freud's and behaviorist John Broadus Watson's influences on child development were not only critical to their time but are still being frequently referenced even today.

THE EARLY TWENTIETH CENTURY

Freud's work focused on the importance of positive early experiences for children, which would help ensure their maturation into becoming well-adjusted adults. With his direction, parents became more aware of the importance of what occurred during these early years than they had ever been before. Whereas parents used to believe that children wouldn't remember things from their early childhood, Freud proposed that these memories were not only crucial but could also determine the kind of adult that the child would grow up to be one day.

Watson approached parenting quite differently from Freud and viewed children as objects that could be molded into becoming well-balanced and productive citizens. Watson's behavioral approach proposed that parenting was almost like a job. Unlike prior generations who felt that children would learn by watching, later studied by Albert Bandura and called *Social Learning Theory*, Watson proposed that a parent could mold a child into what he or she wanted him or her to be.

In contrast to the work of Freud and Watson, the 1930s and 1940s saw a much more relaxed view toward parenting, which started to include some of the joys of parenting.

C. Anderson Aldrich, coauthor of *Babies are Human Beings*, recommended parents acknowledge the emotional and natural development of children (1938). This allowed parents for the first time to truly enjoy being a parent and set the stage for the next chapter of parenting that was readily embraced by the masses.

THE MID-TWENTIETH CENTURY

In 1946, Benjamin Spock's *The Common Sense Book of Baby and Child Care* further reinforced this type of naturalistic approach of Aldrich. In what must have been remarkable for the time, Spock advised parents to trust their own parenting instincts and recommended that they work with their children by trying to understand them. Spock's parenting style was popular during this post–World War II period and had many parents implementing this child-centered approach well into the 1970s. Even today, there are those who favor this naturalistic approach to parenting and have taken some of Spock's concepts into a variety of parenting approaches.

Perhaps one of the most influential researchers who first laid down the foundation for the various types of parenting approaches occurred during the 1960s and 1970s. Researcher and psychologist Diana Baumrind became very popular with her work on the categorization of parents. Based on her research, Baumrind proposed that the three most widely used parenting styles were (1967):

- *The authoritarian parenting style:* This style expanded on the work previously established by Freud. It is characterized by what many parents would consider the old-fashioned approach to parenting where strict rules are expected to be followed by the children. Parents tend to be strict, and children are expected to be obedient.
- *The permissive parenting style:* This category proposed by Baumrind expanded on the work previously completed by Watson. This style is often characterized, in direct contrast to the authoritarian parenting style, by a

lack of and little to no discipline. Despite the love and care that parents may have for their children, they prefer not to accept many of the responsibilities of admonishing and disciplining their children. There is a general lack of rules and those that do exist are not enforced consistently.

- *The authoritative parenting style:* Baumrind described this style as being a combination of both. This parent establishes rules and boundaries for their child and is responsive to his/her needs. This type of parent metes out discipline in a fair and consistent manner and isn't afraid to show love and attention.

Of the three approaches, it is quite obvious that the last approach seems to be the most reasonable approach to raising children.

The 1980s saw a major increase in the number of women entering the workforce and with this a shift in the roles of parents and family structures. These mothers, sometimes referred to as *super moms*, who had previously provided stability in the family for centuries, were now balancing, or attempting to balance, familial and professional responsibilities simultaneously.

Mothers during this time had a difficult time juggling the responsibilities of working and being a mother. It was during this time that parents began having to work more hours, thus spending less time with their children. In addition to that, the rise in divorce also impacted families, thus creating an increase in the familiar configurations such as single parents and blended families.

The 1990s saw the advent of *soccer moms* and *soccer dads*. This generation saw both parents juggling both their professional lives as well as their family responsibilities. To compensate for the decrease in time spent with their children, these parents ensured that every minute outside of work was engaged in some sort of activity with their children, such as soccer games, piano lessons, or school plays. Although a form of it most likely has always been in practice, it appears the increase in the visibility of *hyper-parenting* styles developed during this time.

In the new millennium, parenting in America has become much more of a potpourri of approaches. While much of this could most likely be attributed to the diversity of cultures and lifestyles that exist in the country today, never before have there been more variations of the family structure, which not only include the traditional two-parent family, but large numbers of single parent and blended families as well (Ginther and Pollak, 2004). The new century saw how the social networking of the Information Age has changed how the world shares information and communicates.

Chapter Three

Parenting Styles in the New Millennium

Parenting in the new millennium is indeed a difficult task. Never before in the history of our nation have parents been confronted with the amount of stimuli that is available today.

Think of the variety of different challenges that face parents today:

- Rising divorce rates
- Advancements in technology
- Increase in violence
- Children maturing early
- Economic recession
- Changing family dynamics

Cataloging all of the available parenting styles in our current society is a difficult task mainly because new terms seem to be added on a frequent basis. Whereas in the past parenting advice came only from professionals in the fields of psychology, sociology, or education, today information about best practices in parenting can also come from independent bloggers, advocacy groups on the Internet, and other websites—literally a voice and a platform for everyone and every approach.

Nonetheless, researching all of the existing parenting styles being utilized in the new millennium has resulted in some very interesting findings. In an attempt to better distinguish these styles, the following five broad categories are used for organizational purposes by the author:

- *Hyper-parenting*
- *Hypo-parenting*

- *Traditional/neo-traditional parenting*
- *Millennial parenting*
- *Divergent parenting*

Unless otherwise cited, the terms used in this article are the work of this author based on field experience that includes, but is not limited to, formal and informal meetings, conferences, and conversations with parents, teachers, and other professionals who interact with children of various ages on a daily basis.

The term *hyper-parenting* is based on the work of Alvin Rosenfeld and Nicole Wise from their book, *The Over-Scheduled Child: Avoiding the Hyper-Parenting Trap* (2001). In their book, the authors discuss how some parents tend to micromanage their children's daily lives. Thus, this term is being used here to categorize high energy, over-involved parents who tend to have preset goals for their children and are focused on making them successful, sometimes at any cost. Critics often view these parents as living out their own lives through their children, whereas supporters feel that it is a parent's obligation to ensure that his or her children succeed and to assist them in resolving their conflicts.

Hypo-parenting was used in Rosenfeld and Wise's book as a means to distinguish the type of parenting that leans to a more "hands off" approach. The term *hypo* was chosen to clearly distinguish this approach as characteristically opposite from the previously mentioned *hyper-parenting*. These parents tend to allow children to exercise more control of their own decisions, see the importance of individuality, and are more permissive than other parents.

Traditional/neo-traditional parenting is a style that in many ways is a return to the 1950s/1960s era of parenting. These parents try their best to ensure that one parent assumes the role of the primary caretaker while the other parent is chiefly responsible for the family's financial obligations. In the past, this usually meant that the father worked while the mother stayed at home, whereas today's family may look a little different from that but still maintain the stability of this structure. Although not as ubiquitous as in previous generations, this dynamic still exists today but also includes stay at home parents of both sexes and from nontraditional families.

Millennial parenting is unique to the times in which we live and reflects the complexity of modern life in America. This category encompasses all of the current types of parenting approaches, as well as fads, that do not apply to the previously mentioned styles. In some cases, it could be both parents working full-time who are forced to find nontraditional ways of raising children and in other cases it might include environmentally safe parenting techniques. Although some of the *hyper-* and *hypo-parenting* styles may have recently developed during the new millennium, I have chosen to keep them in their assigned categories because they more accurately represent the similarities that they share with those in the same category.

Divergent parenting refers to parenting styles that would most likely not be recommended by professionals but are included here, not because they should necessarily be emulated by parents, but rather, like it or not, because they exist in our society. Although these approaches are often used out of necessity and are present in more dysfunctional families, insight into these styles can be useful to better understand how to work and interact with children who are products of these environments. Every attempt has been made to *demonize* these parents, but this style is documented for the sake of understanding the wide expanse of parenting approaches that are implemented by the parents of our students.

Chapter Four

Hyper-Parenting

INTRODUCTION

Hyper-parenting, also sometimes referred to as *overparenting* and even *excessive parenting*, is a broad term often used for types of parents who tend to over-involve themselves in many, if not all, aspects of their child's major life activities. These parents will often try to solve all of their children's problems and have been known to micromanage all of their child's decisions, thus preventing them from acquiring problem-solving skills of their own. These parents tend to limit the interactions with other children because it could lead to potential conflicts with other children and even their parents.

When their children are young, these parents will *hover* around them to ensure that there is always some level of supervision occurring at all times. In some cases, even when their children become older, they tend to want to take care of things for their children even well into their college years and beyond. We have all met adults who have had over-involved parents and wondered how that relationship had developed. For many of them, *hyper-parenting* may be responsible for the impetus of these relationships.

Hyper-parenting parents can often be found making many decisions for their children such as their friends, clothing, hobbies, college and academic decisions, or other facets of their life; these decisions can run from the mundane to very important. These parents tend to call the schools quite often, frequently meet or want to meet with teachers and administrators, and want to make nearly all of the decisions for their children.

They sometimes have also been characterized by:

- Over-involvement in even the smallest of decisions
- Blurring the line between their own goals and their children's

- Becoming overly emotional or irrational regarding their children
- Setting overly high expectations for their children
- Becoming violent when other people interfere with their children
- Removing most if not all obstacles from their children's path
- Trying to destroy anyone who comes in the way of raising their children
- Staying involved well into their children's adolescent and adult years
- Losing perspective in situations that involve their own children

Hyper-parenting tends to occur because of a parent's genuine desire to help his/her child but seems to stem from the fact that they may have some insecurities, either about themselves or about their children (i.e., they view their child as having deficiencies that would prevent him/her from succeed-ing in life). In many cases, these parents feel that their children would not succeed if were not for their assistance. In other situations, a *hyper-parent* can even create or exacerbate shortcomings, preventing their children from developing problem-solving skills of their own.

Parents sometimes over-parent because of things that have occurred in their own past that they do not want to see reoccur with their own children. For example, some parents may have felt that they received little attention from their own parents and want to ensure that the same treatment does not occur with them, so they overcorrect their actions to compensate for the fear. In other cases, divorce, childhood illness, or other trauma might have oc-curred that caused these parents to take more control over their children. In one experience, the death of an older sibling led to the parents being more restrictive with their young child. Some recent research has even shown that children from hyper-parents have been shown to be more depressed and dissatisfied with their lives (Goldsmith, 2013).

ATTACHMENT PARENTING

Background

This style includes parents who form strong emotional bonds with their chil-dren, respond immediately to their children's needs, and can be overly atten-tive (McGolerick, 2011). They are always available and often may even put their own lives on hold to ensure that their children are constantly feeling satisfied. These parents usually avoid physical punishment for their children and work on positive instead of negative reinforcement. They seek to holisti-cally understand their children and make their entire lives children-centered. These parents are characterized by a nurturing approach that continues well beyond the child's infancy.

They might also be described as:

- Overindulgent
- Opinionated
- Assertive
- Attentive
- Empathic with their children
- Apprehensive to other's ideas
- Informed

Examples

Attachment parents show their attachments through such actions as co-sleeping, hovering over their children, and constant physical affection. These parents would most likely find it difficult to drop off their children at school and can be found taking a long time to say goodbye before they leave. They will also find reasons to hang around or come back to school like dropping off assignments or forgetting their child's lunch. *Attachment parents* feel that staying in close proximity to their children will better serve them. They cherish time with their children and sometimes can become obsessive.

More recently, *attachment parenting* received a great deal of public attention with the controversial cover of *Time Magazine* that featured an article by Kate Pickert. The cover photo depicted a mother breastfeeding her three-year-old son (2012). Although some were outraged, other parents defended this type of parenting believing that bonding with children makes for healthier more adjusted children.

Some additional examples of behaviors from this particular parenting style might also include the following:

- They may prescribe to the belief that breastfeeding well into toddler years is beneficial for their children.
- Co-sleeping with their children well beyond the toddler years may be present.
- They may overly attend to even the most insignificant of their children's tasks.
- They may find ways to delay their child from assuming age-appropriate responsibilities.
- They may allow excessive baby talk that is not age-appropriate.
- They may display an unhealthy level of attachment anxiety.

Possible Reasoning

These parents feel that strong emotional bonds with their children will ensure strong relationships with them. They may also tend to believe that these strong attachments will help their children become emotionally healthy individuals. In some cases, these parents become so child-centered that they do not seek to further develop themselves or their children.

There are no doubt benefits parents receive from forming attachments to their children but as with all of the styles covered in this book, when the parenting becomes excessive or obsessive it ceases to be a productive form of child rearing. For some parents, focusing just on their children might even provide them an excuse from addressing their own shortcomings or personal development. Other parents might not even consider themselves overly attached to their children and would refuse to categorize themselves as such.

Teachers might often hear the following things from these parents:

- "I think that bonding is the most important part of parenting."
- "I want to be more independent with him but he just misses me too much so that's why I hang around."
- "She can't do it on her own. She needs my help."
- "I want him to know that I'm always here for him."

How Educators Could Best Work with These Parents

Educators could best work with this parenting style by understanding that these parents can never get enough information and updates about their children and what they are doing in the classroom. They love to volunteer and can be very assistive with field trips, activities, and school programs. They will always try to find ways to get involved in class projects and field trips, and so their involvement should be put to constructive purposes. They will also not like to hear critical analysis of their children's progress but will be generally receptive to it. Teachers should establish clear ground rules in the beginning of the year by limiting the length and types of contact that is permissible within their class.

A teacher might also:

- Establish clear class learning objectives and make them accessible to parents.
- Be sensitive and listen carefully, critically, and reflectively to parent concerns and complaints. What might start out as sounding like a complaint could turn into a plea for help or some useful information that could be beneficial to better understanding the student.
- Make sure that in meeting with these parents that you have a sufficient amount of examples and evidence to support what you want to share with them. Sometimes generalization is helpful and other times specificity is needed to illustrate a point.

BLACKHAWK PARENTS

Background

The title refers to the assault helicopters used by the US military to wage attacks against opposing forces. In some cases, from the *Blackhawk parents'* perspective, this could be doctors, teachers, neighbors, or even other family members who they feel pose some type of threat to their children (Coll, 2007). These parents are more aggressive than other *hyper-parents* in ensuring that their children are protected from anything that might be unpleasant or even critical. They step so far over the line that they engage in unethical behavior for their child, such as writing term papers, completing science projects, or completing their children's homework.

They might also be described as:

- Excessive
- Mistrusting of other adults as well as educational professionals
- Aggressive
- Overly protective

Examples

Blackhawk parents will often view teachers who are critical of their children as their enemies. They may verbally attack teachers or any other educator who stands in their way or provides even the slightest bit of criticism regarding their child. They tend to have very close-knit families that are very cohesive and are extremely protective of each other. When this protectiveness becomes excessive, they can be confrontational and adversarial to teachers and staff members. *Blackhawk parents* are always on the lookout for potential threats and are not overly concerned if their fears are legitimate or not. Their priority is their children and they take it very seriously—even if it harms someone else.

Some additional examples of behaviors from this particular parenting style might include:

- Doing their children's homework for them and becoming belligerent if someone accuses them of doing it
- Confronting their children's peers to settle their disputes instead of allowing their children the opportunity to do it for themselves
- Engaging in fights with other adults about their children, causing tension and resentment
- Turning their children against other adults through their words, comments, and opinions

Possible Reasoning

In my experience with parents from this category, it appears that their actions are based on their need to protect their children, or more accurately overprotect them. This may stem from their own insecurities or perhaps it may have developed from some event from their past that has happened to them. I have witnessed these types of parents violently confront teachers to prevent their children from experiencing any disappointment and in the process make the event much more of a spectacle than necessary. They take criticisms of their children as personal insults and will react harshly. They will ensure that their children are not targeted by teacher, their children's peers, or other adults, and tend to strike out before anyone has an opportunity to criticize their children.

Teachers might often hear the following things from these parents:

- "You don't know what's best for my child, I do."
- "You just don't like my child. That's why you're picking on her."
- "I want that other kid punished as well. I refuse to believe my child isn't telling the truth!"
- "I don't think he deserves to be disciplined. That's supposed to be our job as parents, not yours."

How Educators Could Best Work with These Parents

Setting clear lines of communication and establishing boundaries is always helpful in working with these parents. Being prepared, keeping open lines of communication, and staying on top of things helps to create positive working relationships with these parents. At times, it might be necessary to seek the advice of fellow colleagues or administrators for certain meetings to help maintain order and focus. A teacher should not always assume a *Blackhawk parent's* behavior is malevolent. Most often, from the parent's perspective, he or she feels that protecting his or her children, at any expense, is a parent's obligation. It is critical to help these parents understand that constrictive criticism is an important part of the educational process and is done so that students can grow and be successful.

A teacher might also:

- Keep good student records that include homework, phone and parent contacts, class participation tests grades and performance, as well as how well the child is performing in relationship to the rest of the class.
- Be proactive. Try to contact these parents before a problem arises or immediately when it occurs. It's always better to hear bad news from the teacher and not have the student tell the parent first. Unfortunately, stu-

dents can leave out crucial information that preys on these parents' over-protective character.

- In meeting with these parents, make sure to have a sufficient amount of examples and evidence to support what you want to share with them. These parents do not like to hear generalizations. The descriptions of the inappropriate behaviors should be factual and explained with as little emotion as possible.

COMMANDO PARENTS

Background

The title of this particular parenting style refers to the behaviors that these parents exhibit that have many similarities to military drill sergeants (Elmore, 2011). They maintain tight control over their children, enforce strict rules, and impose severe consequences. Children are expected to follow these rules and adhere to their parents' commands at all times, whether they are at home, school, or anywhere else. There is little room for negotiations or child input into discussions with these parents. This is a top-down management style where children follow the orders of the parents and act accordingly in all situations.

When moderately used, problems seldom present themselves in the classroom. But in extreme cases, children live in constant fear of their parents and struggle to live up to their parents' high expectations. This dictatorial approach is also much easier to enforce in the younger years but as children mature into adolescence I have witnessed some family conflicts that have occurred attributed to power struggles. Because of these high expectations, sometimes the children may suffer from anxiety, frustration, and low self-esteem.

They might also be described as:

- Aggressive
- Mistrusting of many other adults
- Well-organized
- Having a low threshold for failure

Examples

These are the types of parents who can be seen yelling at their children in public if they happen to lose a game, make a mistake, or show weakness. *Commando parents* are also the types of parents who don't mind piling on additional responsibilities for their children and will go to great lengths to eradicate as much perceived "weakness" from their children as they can. As coaches, these parents will expect their children to surpass the other players. As parents, they demand compliance and obedience. These parents tend to be the ones who become so emotional at sporting events that they are thrown out or suspended from attending games. At the very core of this parenting model is control, and the emotional repercussions of the children are not given priority.

Some additional examples of behaviors from this particular parenting style might also include:

- Embarrassing their children in front of their teachers and peers
- Placing too much emphasis on attaining certain milestones and recognition for their children
- Putting too much blame on their children for the mistakes they make
- Becoming confrontational with other adults when it comes to their children
- Placing pressure and high expectations on their children

Possible Reasoning

Generally speaking, in my experience when working with parents who tend to be extreme, as is the case with *hyper-parents* or *hypo-parents*, I have found some reoccurring patterns. These parents usually either were raised in a similar manner or their actions are the polar opposite of their own childhoods.

For example, when discussing the progress of one of my former students with her father, who could be described as a *commando parent*, he related to me that he was raised with few rules and little restrictions. Although he enjoyed this freedom growing up, he felt that it really hampered him later in life as an adult. He revealed to me that it took many years before he was able to develop the self-discipline that was need to be successful in life. He vowed that he would provide much more structure and order into his own daughter's life to help her become successful.

Teachers might often hear the following things from these parents:

- "That's not his best. He can do better and don't let him tell you anything other than that."
- "I don't tolerate weakness from my children."
- "She will never be a problem for you in class. I can promise you that much."
- "We expect our son to follow our rules at home as well as your rules in the classroom."

How Educators Could Best Work with These Parents

These parents tend to be extremely strict and their children will most often be very respectful and obedient students. In discussions with my elementary school colleagues, these children usually are very respectful and the mere threat of calling their parents will immediately cease any disruptive behavior. These parents are very by the book and will often know the policies and procedures of the school district by heart. But as children of these parents mature, friction between them can develop, especially in the middle and secondary grades. At this level, I have experienced very turbulent situations that sometimes include violence or children running away. Additionally, *commando parents* can become abusive to their children in some situations, and as with all students, teachers should always be on the lookout for signs of abuse or neglect.

A teacher might also:

- Establish a clear code of conduct in the classroom, which does not conflict with the school handbook or any district policies, that details actions and timelines.
- Be firm, fair, and consistent with every student, especially when administering discipline.
- Try not to give too much information that could confuse the purpose of a parent meeting. Sometimes in trying to provide too many examples, a conversation can veer off into a different direction than what you initially wanted.
- Set a specific agenda for a parent meeting and try your best to stick with it. Try not to jump from one topic to another. In many cases although much is discussed, nothing is ever resolved.
- Try not to feed into the emotions of parents who can be overly critical of their children. Parents can sometimes be manipulative and will find ways for teachers to buy into their philosophies.
- Implement a specific action plan for the student with detailed expectations and deadlines.

CURLING PARENTS

Background

This term was first coined by Danish psychologist Bent Hougaard when he noticed how some parents exhibited the same strategies in child rearing as the Olympic winter sport of *curling*. In this event, two people equipped with brooms sweep the obstacles off the ice for the curl to move successfully toward the targeted area (Hougaard, 2004). Teammates sweep the ice so that the curl has a better chance of getting to the right spot.

Much like *lawnmower parenting*, which will be covered later, these parents are more sophisticated and will smooth the way for their children so that they encounter few, if any, challenges during their childhood. They would much rather do everything they possibly can for their child and remove as many roadblocks as possible so that the child experiences as little anxiety as possible.

Although all parents generally try to reduce the anxiety levels of their children, *curling parents* are excessive and seek to ameliorate nearly all of their children's struggles because they feel that it will improve their children's lives. Despite their own pressures and obstacles, these parents put their children first and dedicate themselves to providing as trouble-free an experience as they can for their children.

They might also be described as:

- Overly compensatory
- Excuse makers
- Enablers
- Crafty
- Overly attentive
- Potentially confrontational

Examples

Curling parents can be found at all ages and grade levels. She could be the parent who stays up all night just to finish her son's term paper, or he could be a father who prevents his daughter from resolving a dispute with another child. Whatever the obstacle is, these parents will look to address it for their children. They act with confidence and will not be afraid to rationalize their actions to other adults or even teachers. They will find ways to remove obstacles like due dates from class by providing fallacious doctor's notes or even calling the child out sick from school.

Some additional examples of behaviors from this particular parenting style might also include:

- Staying up late to complete their child's project even though he/she should be doing it
- Making excuses for their children's missing assignments and looking for loopholes to get extensions or remove penalties
- Calling their child out on a day of a test because he or she didn't study for a test that is scheduled

- Defending their children when they are obviously wrong, sometimes even to the point of bullying other people until they relent

Possible Reasoning

There have been some *curling parents* who have shared with me some information that provides insight into some of their behaviors. For instance, their own parents never supported anything they did and thus their childhood was wrought with struggle and anxiety. Others have confided that their parents acted in much the same manner and are not even aware that there is an alternate way of raising children. In any event, this leads them to making sure that it doesn't occur with their own children.

Curling parents are very sensitive about this issue and do not see anything wrong with what they perceive as helping their children. They may also see that any parent that does not do similar things is not as caring as they are. They devote a lot of time to making sure that their children suffer as little as possible in their lives because they feel that decreasing anxiety will enhance their childhoods.

Teachers might often hear the following things from these parents:

- "He wasn't able to do the whole thing by himself. That's why I had to finish it for him."
- "I know she knows how to do it, so why bother with her doing it again on a quiz?"
- "Sure, we helped him with it, but not that much. He did almost all of it himself."
- "I don't think your directions were clear enough to the students."

How Educators Could Best Work with These Parents

It is always advisable that teachers try to create projects and assignments that allow for full student participation and limit the amount of parental assistance. In other cases, teachers can even create supplemental assignments that actually encourage parent participation. To develop student independence, teachers can have children be able to explain the step-by-step procedures to discourage these parents from giving too much help.

Another suggestion would be, where age appropriate, to provide guidelines for how parents can and cannot help their children with their homework and assignments with rationales regarding how it would impact the learning process. In addition, teachers could provide lessons on conflict resolution as part of character development. It is a good suggestion for teachers to provide parents of children of any age skills such as those outlined in *Partnership for*

Twenty-First Century Skills (2004), which highlight problem solving and critical thinking.

A teacher might also:

- Establish clear class learning objectives and make them accessible to parents.
- Make information available to parents about regarding tests, projects, and quizzes that include classroom expectations. If possible, provide as detailed a rubric as possible.
- Be proactive. Try to contact these parents before a problem arises or immediately when one does occur.
- Provide examples of what successful projects and presentations look like and post them in the classroom and on your website if available.
- Allow students an opportunity to reflect on all of their presentations and include a self-assessment that includes the opportunity for students to critically think how they could improve their work.

GROUPIE PARENTS

Background

Although they share some similarities with the *best friend parents*, *groupie parents* can be described as parents whose adoration and high regard extend way beyond the norm (Elmore, 2011). These parents sometimes take on a nearly sycophant relationship with their children that teeters on being unhealthy. In direct opposition to a *tiger mom*, these parents are so enamored by their own children that they fail to see any flaw and will not take seriously anyone who does, especially if it comes from one of the teachers.

What also makes this style confusing is that it is very difficult for the child to understand which accomplishments are real and which ones are just exaggerated by the parents. In many cases, the children grow up with a false sense of accomplishment and very seldom receive any criticism from anyone except their teachers.

These parents might also be described as:

- Overly attentive
- Overly supportive
- Myopic
- Shallow
- Optimistic

Examples

Although all parents can have a tendency to see only the good characteristics of their children, these *groupie parents* turn a blind eye to anything that is perceived by others a negative. In fact, these parents will even turn the negative characteristics of the children into opportunities to celebrate them as victories. For example, I have witnessed parents who bragged about the number of suspensions their child received, touting their prowess in driving the teachers crazy. In that situation, the child was credited for having the most suspensions recorded in the family's history.

Another characteristic of *groupie parents* is their tendency to talk and brag about their children. If given the opportunity, they will detail every aspect of the child's life, including every milestone and accolade the child has ever accomplished in life. Their houses may display hundreds of their children's pictures plastered on every piece of available wall space. And when the children eventually leave for college or to live on their own, their rooms become shrines that are meticulously maintained for any unsuspecting visitor who will be given the full tour.

Some additional examples of behaviors from this particular parenting style might also include the following:

- Conversations always reference their children or will relate back to something they have accomplished or in the process of accomplishing.
- They are never able to critically view their children under any circumstances. They always find their children to be absolutely wonderful and free of any flaws.
- *Groupie parents* will be overly obsessive when it comes to matters regarding their children and do things like collect artifacts that include every piece of writing or artwork completed by their children.

Possible Reasoning

Most parents are generally supportive of their children's endeavors, but *groupie parents* are extreme in their actions. Because of their near obsession with their children, they do not see potential problems that can arise because of their never-ending cheerleading. In some cases, I believe that these behaviors may start out well intended with parents feeling the need to support their children. But if not carefully monitored, this excessive behavior can produce some unattractive behaviors in the children that could prevent them from fostering productive relationships with their peers. Lastly, the unrealistic assessments of their children can backfire on the parents because their children quickly realize that the world will not be as kind and considerate with their emotions as their parents have been.

Teachers might often hear the following things from these parents:

- "He's unlike any other ten-year-old that I have ever seen."
- "I'm sure that you have already noticed by now, but my son is very advanced."
- "I don't think you see his potentials like I do."
- "He's so talented. It's unbelievable."
- "I could just look at his drawings all day if I could."

How Educators Could Best Work with These Parents

It's the excessive praise that these parents pour on their children that poses the biggest challenge in the classroom. Because they are so used to attention and praise, they may not feel like they are getting sufficient adulations in a class where there are fifteen to twenty other students. This can create some feelings of inadequacy for these students as they begin to realize that the world can be quite an unassuming place.

In most cases, even the *groupie parent*'s excessiveness begins to dissipate as the child ages throughout school. When they reach their teenager years, for the most part, the parents are not as prominent in the day-to-day affairs of the children. In addition, most teens are much more interested in what their peers tend to think of them than their parents. I have, however, seen an increase in the number of *groupie parents* at the secondary level. I think that some of the independence that was once afforded high school students is slightly changing. I have witnessed many more parents remaining overly connected with their teenagers than ever before in my career.

A teacher might also:

- Be firm, fair, and consistent with these parents and establish that a teacher's role is to help children become better. In some cases, that may mean that sometimes teachers will have to offer constructive criticism.
- Do not be afraid to professionally disagree with the parent. Although the phrase, "Let's agree to disagree" has become quite cliché, it is a reality. The goal of every parent meeting should be to reach some sort of agreement but there will always be the outliers where agreement just is not possible. Know when a conversation is going around in circles and move on to the next topic.
- Take notes during parent meetings. Sometimes even the smallest or seemingly most insignificant things that are said at these meetings will be brought up at a later time.
- Have a specific set of things you are willing to offer the parents (i.e., extra help, additional assignments, make-up work, daily or weekly contacts, etc.).

- Always be professional. Sometimes it is difficult not to give our opinions about things but in the long run it just isn't worth it. It's good to remember that when parents sometimes ask for our opinion they really don't want it unless it is favorable. Keeping focused on being professional is always best.

HELICOPTER PARENTS

Background

This type of parenting has gained wide notoriety and was first described in Foster Cline and Jim Fay's work in 1990 for parents who are always hovering over their children. These parents are characterized by their over-involvement; they limit the amount of decisions made by the individual child to where the parents solve almost all of their children's problems for them.

The term derives from the fact that these parents tend to "hover" around their children. like a helicopter. constantly supervising their children. Unfortunately, this prevents children from developing problem-solving skills that will benefit them in later in their lives.

This is perhaps one of the most dominant types of *hyper-parenting* and is even allowed or encouraged to a certain degree. Although they can pose some challenges to educators, they tend to have the best intentions for their children and are not as destructive as some other styles in this category.

They might also be described as:

- Always needing more information and never satisfied with what they are given
- Eager to participate in as many school and community activities as possible
- Needing constant attention from the teacher or any adult who interacts with their child
- Requiring immediate feedback

Examples

These parents prefer to be constantly within close proximity and earshot of their children and will intervene at the slightest provocation from another child or adult. These parents have the hardest time when their children begin school and will find countless ways to find excuses to see them during the day such as "forgetting" a snack or homework assignment. *Helicopter parents* will attend every sporting event and school function their child is involved in. What separates this parent from others is that they will intervene and often direct the school professional as to what to do differently. *Helicop-*

ter parents have no problem telling a teacher he or she is wrong or correcting a coach's decision. They do not have a tendency to want to encourage their children to solve any of their problems and will instead see why every other child is wrong and theirs is right.

Some additional examples of behaviors from this particular parenting style might also include:

- Finding ways to stay in the school even after they drop off their children to school
- Reminding everyone else how much they attend everything and putting down parents who do not participate
- Never finding any fault in their own children but finding plenty with other people's children
- Attacking and being confrontational with other students and teachers if necessary

Possible Reasoning

As with most parents in this category, their intentions are genuine in that they have the desire to protect their children like most other parents do. It becomes excessive when their actions impact their children's social and emotional development. Their need to ensure that their children are academically and socially successful sometimes gets in the way of good common sense and allowing their children to develop naturally on their own.

In discussions with some *helicopter parents*, I have found that many of them have developed a distrust of the public education system that actually fuels their behavior to oversee every detail of their children's time in school. In other cases, these parents sometimes had such negative experiences with school in their own pasts that they have become watchdogs to ensure that the same things aren't done to their own children.

I remember one case: a parent vehemently wanted her child moved from a class even though it was not recommended by the school administration. As the discussion became very heated, the parent actually slipped and accused the administrator of not allowing her to leave a class when she was a child. It was then that the administrator knew that this was not a case of where the student felt threatened but that the mother's negative experience in her own past made her much more sensitive than other parents.

Teachers might often hear the following things from these parents:

- "I need to be constantly updated on what he's doing."
- "I just care more than the other parents."
- "His other teachers called me every week. I don't see why you can't do the same."

- "Other parents should care as much as we do."
- "I don't care what you do with the other students, my son is different."

How Educators Could Best Work with These Parents

Educators could benefit by establishing productive lines of communication with *helicopter parents*. Teachers should listen carefully and make any arrangements that are possible that would allow all parents to exchange information regarding the progress of their children. Sometimes it can be very difficult to listen to these parents because they have the potential to be rude but every once in a while a little piece of information can be found that leads to a better understanding of the parent as well as the student. In one situation, a student's reading disability had been covered up so well that it wasn't until something the parent accidently said something that the teacher was able to help the student.

These parents are very organized and attentive, and they expect to be updated on a frequent basis. By establishing student, teacher, and parent expectations in the beginning of the school year, teachers can use this as the guidelines for productive interactions.

A teacher might also do the following:

- In scheduling conferences, make sure to predetermine the topic, or topics, to discuss, the location, and the approximate length of the meeting. In cases where parents do not always respect these guidelines, ask a colleague to contact you at specific time as a reminder to conclude the meeting.
- Maintain excellent student records that include homework, phone and parent contacts, class participation tests grades, and performance. Knowing how well the child is performing in relationship to the rest of the class or classes can be beneficial to better understanding his or her progress and potential.
- In meeting with these parents, make sure to have a sufficient amount of examples and evidence to support what you want to share with them. Be prepared for the parent meeting and make sure that you have all records and information that you think you will need.
- Reflect on prior conversations that you have had and make sure that all items from previous meetings have been addressed. If they haven't, make sure to have reasons why.
- Try not to promise something that might not be possible to deliver. Make realistic expectations and goals.

INVESTMENT PARENTING

Background

This particular style was presented in Bryan Caplan's book, *Selfish Reasons to Have More Kids: Why Being a Great Parent is Less Work and More Fun Than You Think* (2012). Caplan explained that some parents wish to live out their own goals through their children and will do so at any cost. *Investment parents* do not always recognize their motivations, although they may be obvious to everyone else around them. The author goes on to advise that investing too much energy may actually be counterproductive in raising children.

Investment parents sometimes believe that the struggles they faced in their pasts could be overcome by carefully supervising their own children and guiding them to the path of success. Most often in my experience with students, these *investments* have occurred in the areas of athletics, academics, popularity, and overall success. They are very attentive and will monitor their children's progress and contact the school when they feel an opportunity is not being properly pursued for their child.

They might also be described as:

- Self-centered
- Over-involved
- Excessive
- Displaying a disregard for children's own individuality
- Maintaining a loss of perspective

Examples

Sometimes these parents can be found vehemently questioning the decisions of teachers and coaches in public. Perhaps they disapprove of how something is done on the playing field or even in the classroom. They may also not understand the reason why their child is not starting the game or being recommended for advanced classes even though they may not exhibit the qualifications to do so. These parents tend to see the potential of their children and not acknowledge the reality of their performance. In other instances, their children may already be high-achievers but the parents want to give their children the edge through whatever means necessary.

Some additional examples of behaviors from this particular parenting style might also include:

- Forcing their children to attend events that the children don't necessarily want to go to just because the parents feel it will somehow benefit the children later in life
- Making their children enter contests and competitions the children are not necessarily interested in entering
- Starting their children at very early ages in a particular area or field of study
- Publicly telling everyone what their child's future will be

Possible Reasoning

These parents feel that with the proper guidance they can ensure that their children will achieve the levels of success expected of them. They are firm believers that early direction in a child's life can propel them toward success—providing examples of child prodigies on demand is one of their greatest attributes.

Perhaps they reflect on their own pasts and see how proper direction could have benefited them more and given them greater success than what they achieved. They may also see potential in their own children and feel that no one is better qualified than themselves in guiding their children to success. These parents will devote hours to ensure that their children are the best at whatever they are pursuing, sometimes even giving up parts of their own lives to better prepare their children.

In other cases, children are often pressured to participate in things purely because it is the wishes of their parents. This poses problems because the children can often rebel during their adolescences, which could spill over into the classroom.

Teachers might often hear the following things from these parents:

- "I want him to have all of the advantages that I never had."
- "I wish my parents put as much time and effort as we are doing with her. I would have been a lot better off."
- "No one ever realized my potential until it was too late. I won't let that happen with my child."
- "We can't just rely on the school system to help him succeed."
- "He should be the captain of the team!"

How Educators Could Best Work with These Parents

These parents can be very difficult to convince that the ambitious plans they have for their children can sometimes be counterproductive. They believe that their actions are well-intended and will not let anyone, educational professionals, fellow family members, or even their spouses, tell them otherwise. They will hold fiercely to their beliefs and can become volatile if they feel that someone is trying to veer them away from their goal.

In some cases, I have had parents fight for their children to be enrolled in honors and advanced classes, against the recommendation of teachers and counselors, only to have the child fail as a result. Of course, there have also been several times where the student excelled as well. Sometimes it can be quite difficult to fully ascertain if a parent is being overly influential or just supportive. If at all possible, it is often necessary to allow these children opportunities to excel while still advising the parents of the ramifications.

A teacher might also:

- Be proactive. Try to contact these parents before a problem arises or immediately when it does occur.
- Be sensitive and listen carefully, critically, and reflectively to parent concerns and complaints. What might start out as sounding like a complaint may turn into useful information that could better help the student achieve.
- Reflect on prior conversations and be careful what you say. These parents tend to remember every word and will reference it when it is needed for their argument.
- Be understanding to what the parent and the student want to do. In many cases, the parent will provide additional and supplemental aid if they think that it will benefit their child.

LAWNMOWER PARENTING

Background

Lori Borgman explained in her article that this style, which on the surface is very similar to *curling parenting*, is characterized by parents mowing down obstacles to ensure better chances for their children to succeed; it differs from *curling parenting* in a few vital ways (2011). These parents also are known to complete their children's homework assignments and projects, and make it appear that it was completed on their own. At other times, they might provide excuses for their children when deadlines aren't met and create elaborate stories to cover up their child's mistake. They are not as refined in their tactics as *curling parents*, who at least make attempts to curtail their overinvolvement in their children's affairs. Their cover-ups are usually haphazardly put together and quite transparent.

They might also be described as:

- Determined
- Overly attentive
- Crafty

- Organized
- Focused

Examples

These parents tend to be much more obvious with their tactics and less refined than the *curling parents* that were previously covered. They do not seem to care what other parents or teachers think about their parenting techniques and have a tendency to push clumsily through obstacles that confront their children. Much like the *curling parents*, they will complete assignments for their children but are often easily found out. When confronted in situations like these, they can be confrontational and argumentative. These parents will sometimes fake doctor's appointments or dates just to remove their children from things they might not want to participate in. For example, if their child doesn't want to attend the physical fitness test that day, they will invent an excuse for their child to be absent. Unlike some of the other parenting styles, *curling parents* directly involve their children in these fabrications.

Some additional examples of behaviors from this particular parenting style might also include:

- Arguing over the smallest details on tests, projects, and assignments just to improve their child's grades
- Disputing any disciplinary actions that their children receives in school and providing excuses and explanations for their actions and misbehavior
- Questioning a teacher's actions, whether it be instructional, organizational, or professional
- Moving up the school's hierarchy to get what they want accomplished if they feel that they are not being responded to promptly enough

Possible Reasoning

In working with these types of parents, I have found that their need for intervening in their children's lives sometimes stems from a genuine desire to provide them with advantages that they perceive their other peers having. This can sometimes mean financial opportunities, academic advantages, or just the political capital of having the right connections to move ahead in the world.

They see their actions as their parental obligation as well as a way to ensure that their children will have the opportunity to succeed. These advantages that they see in other families may be real or perceived. In any event, their general philosophy is one in which success doesn't rely on the individual but rather the advantages that one is given.

Teachers might often hear the following things from these parents:

- "How do they expect kids to do these problems by themselves without the parents helping them?"
- "This is too much homework!"
- "She has a right to have her weekends free to play with her friends."
- "I will do that for you."

How Educators Could Best Work with These Parents

Lawnmower parents mostly aren't afraid or embarrassed when their actions have been discovered. Therefore, teachers should not feel that "outing" them will cease their activity or curb their behaviors. Teachers would be advised to monitor student progress and ensure that all assignments and projects completed at home are done by the student. This can be done in a variety of ways such as using reflection logs, oral presentations, or constructing activities that discourage adult assistance. These parents can pose some challenges but good old-fashioned organizational skills will definitely decrease the number of negative interactions.

A teacher might also do the following:

- In meeting with these parents, make sure to have a sufficient amount of examples and evidence to support what you want to share with them.
- Be prepared for the parent meeting and make sure that you have all records and information that you think you will need.
- Reflect on prior conversations and be careful what you say. These parents tend to remember every word and will reference it when needed.
- Be firm, fair, and consistent.
- Do not be afraid to professionally disagree with the parent. Although the phrase, "Let's agree to disagree" has become quite cliché, it is a reality. The goal of every parent meeting should be to reach some sort of agreement but there will always be the outliers where agreement just is not possible. Know when a conversation is going around in circles and move on to the next topic.

PERMISSIVE PARENTING

Background

Permissive parenting, also sometimes called *indulgent parenting,* stems from the influential work of Diana Baumrind from the 1960s. These parents make relatively few demands of their children and generally have low expectations of self-control and responsibility. They will make excuses for their children and rarely discipline them if they are ever caught doing anything wrong. These lenient parents tend to avoid confrontation and are overly accommodating to their children, granting as many requests as possible for them.

These parents can sometimes be run ragged by attending every event and making sure they play a prominent role in the organization. There are some similarities with the *yes mothers* and *best friend parents*, but differ in that these parents says yes because they have a desire to fulfill every one of their child's wishes and are not interested in being a friend but rather a magical genie of sorts that grants wishes. They spend an inordinate amount of energy trying to make their children happy and are often found to be in a worn state.

They might also be described as:

- Over-indulgent
- Excessive
- Ignorant of personal boundaries
- Materialistic
- Overly accommodating

Examples

These parents over-indulge their children and put relatively few restrictions on them. These parents are easily identifiable because they will allow their children to eat chocolate for breakfast or stay up late on school nights. They make every attempt to purchases the latest and greatest gadgets and toys so that their children have everything they desire. *Permissive parents* will overlook bad behaviors from their children and allow them to act as they wish without any correction.

These parents can be found attending all of their children events and sporting events. They can easily be spotted during birthday parties as the parent who goes well beyond normal activities to include a clown, a horse, a magician, and the entire cast of *Dora the Explorer*.

Some additional examples of behaviors from this particular parenting style might also include:

- Allowing their children to get tattoos before they are 18 years old by going with them and "supervising" the entire thing
- Permitting their children to wear outrageous outfits and hairstyles to school that cause disruptions and being belligerent if they are questioned by school authorities
- Will seldom impose curfews or restrictions on where they go and who they spend their time with
- Will "overlook" drinking parties at their house feeling that pseudo-supervision is better than none at all

Possible Reasoning

All parents can be permissive to a certain extent but the problem with this style occurs when parents are overly indulgent with their children. In some cases, these parents may use money while in other situations I have witnessed the parents are more behaviorally permissive. Seldom will these children hear the word "No," from their parents, and they will expect to be treated the same by every other adult in their lives.

These parents feel that they are doing the right thing in how they address their children and want to provide as many things to them as humanly possible. In some cases, this may be because of feelings of guilt due to work schedules and lack of time spent at home. In other cases, these children may be the products of divorce. Therefore, granting them everything they want may be a way of addressing feelings of guilt by the parents. These parents can also be nurturing and communicative with their children but become blinded by their desire to not disappoint their children, to the point that they are unable to give any criticism (McGolerick, 2011).

Teachers might often hear the following things from these parents:

- "She deserves all of things that I can provide for her."
- "I know parents who provide more things than I do!"
- "Why say no when I don't have to?"
- "I work so that they can have everything they want."

How Educators Could Best Work with These Parents

Children of *permissive parents* can sometimes cause the greatest disruptions in the classroom. Because they are used to getting their way, these children may become difficult when they are denied things or reprimanded by staff. Although this may not always be the case, I have also noticed that sometimes these students, who are permitted by their parents in most things, eventually realize that teachers will not engage in this behavior.

Teachers are recommended to make clear rules in the beginning of the school year, detailing actions and specific consequences. They must make sure that they are consistent with meting out their discipline and ensure that they are treating all students fairly. They may sometimes be confronted with requests by the parents to reconsider decisions but are encouraged to remain firm and fair.

A teacher might also:

- Be proactive. Try to contact these parents before a problem arises or immediately when it does occur.
- Try to use language that addresses the student's specific behavior and not something that can be interpreted as critiquing the parent.

- Do not engage the parents in discussions regarding how other teachers in the past or present worked with their child. You can, however, ask how another teacher was successful in addressing specific behaviors or areas of need.
- Teachers are reminded that all criticism of students should be objective and based on performance.

SNOW PLOW PARENTING

Background

This is yet another variation of *curling* and *lawnmower parenting*, which were covered previously. Much as detailed before, these parents also seek to diminish their child's obstacles and decrease their frustration but this style clearly emphasizes the need for accomplishments, rewards, and recognition. *Snow plow parents* will go to great lengths to ensure that their children not have to work for success, and they will find alternate means to ensure their children's success, making sure the children get acknowledgment in the process (Sze, 2013).

They will use their power, money, or influence to improve their children's chances of success either overtly or covertly. They have no problem with these shallow victories and in some cases make their children believe they actually earned the accolades that they have received.

They might also be described as:

- Ambitious
- Crafty
- Deceptive
- Devious
- Overly attentive

Examples

These parents go way beyond selling cookies for their children's fundraisers so that they can earn a modest prize. They also aren't the parents who hire a Spanish tutor because their son's grades slip to a B in his class. These parents can be deceptive and may give the appearance that their children are actually the ones doing the work while all along behind the scenes they may be the ones who are doing everything.

Snow plow parents are extreme in their ways and will not let ethics or even the law get in the way of making their children succeed. For example, these parents might get involved in school committees just so that they gain influence so that they can have teachers treat their children more favorably.

In other examples, they may use their influence in the community to intimidate school administration.

Some additional examples of behaviors from this particular parenting
style might also include:

- Write essays for their children and have them take credit for it
- Not discipline their child if he/she was found cheating
- Talk badly in public about other students competing against their children
- Find errors with the teachers when their children don't win or excel in a
  subject

Possible Reasoning

As is the case with other parenting styles, *snow plow parents* may pursue this
style because it is familiar to them and taken from their own childhood. It is
often the case that many parents find that the way they were raised is the
best, or even the only, way to raise a child.

They may have seen the benefits to having parents over-involve themselves in their lives and wish to afford their children in the same manner. In
other cases, these parents may be individuals who view winning as extremely
important and will do anything to guarantee that their children are winners.

Teachers might often hear the following things from these parents:

- "My daughter *deserves* to be the class president!"
- "If I need to go to the mayor, I will!"
- "What do we have to do to have my son get that scholarship?"
- "Is there anything I can do to put him in first place?"

How Educators Could Best Work with These Parents

Teachers can usually identify these students because they tend to be high
achievers in many different categories, such as academics, athletics, and
extracurricular activities. Sometimes they may be high-performing and really
don't need their parents' influence, while in other cases their parents' influence is what gives them that needed push to becoming number one or maintaining their status. These parents will also spend quite a bit of their resources
on finding supplemental programs that will help them accomplish their goals
for their children. Teachers will often find themselves in battles over the
smallest things with these parents.

A teacher might also:

- Speak in the positive when possible. A teacher can say the same things in
  a positive way instead of presenting them in the negative one.

- Maintain the mantra that this parent loves his or her child and believes that everything he or she does is because it will benefit the child. Despite what some of the methods might be, *snow plow parents* use blinders when it comes to their family and everyone else. This does not exonerate their actions, but sometimes it is important to remember how misguided people can be.
- Know when to ask for an outside perspective such as a veteran teacher, a supervisor, or an administrator. These parents can be tricky and speak with such confidence that they may intimidate a new teacher to the point where the truth is distorted.

TIGER MOMS (AND DADS)

Background

Amy Chua received some criticism, as well as much praise, for her book about *tiger moms*, published in 2011. Chua relied on her own Asian culture as the foundation for this strict, no-nonsense parenting style that promotes excellence and perfection in children but has also been described by some critics as too aggressive. Proponents of this approach see that the way to ensuring success in this country is through hard work and becoming highly competitive. They view the schools as giving too much credit for participation and feel that children must be pushed to achieve at the highest levels.

This type of parenting motivates children to excel and does not believe in settling for mediocrity. These parents do not give their children praise for mediocre efforts and push them to do better. These parents also do not feel that schools provide enough challenges for children and therefore will increase the rigor for their children in a variety of different ways. They want their children to be well-rounded individuals who excel in a variety of different areas including academics, athletics, and the arts.

They might also be described as:

- Excessive
- Overly attentive
- Strict
- Highly motivated

Examples

Tiger parents set high expectations for their children and unlike other *hyper-parents*, such as *snow plow parents*, they expect their children to do all of the hard work themselves. They push their children to excel academically, athletically, and socially. They enroll them in a variety of activities that promote a well-rounded education that includes academics as well as the arts. It is not unusual to see children of *tiger parents* excelling in music, dance, and theater as well as on various sports teams. In addition to all of these extracurricular activities, they also excel academically in the classroom.

These parents push for their child to succeed and will not give praise until they are satisfied that their child has reached his or her full potential. They get upset if their child gets below an A and will monitor the online grade-book on a daily basis. In most cases, pressure is put on the child and not the teacher. They do not blame the education system for any shortcomings of their children but will always seek to supplement education with activities outside the school. These parents are strict rule followers themselves and will actually read the school handbooks as well as its corresponding rules and procedures.

Some additional examples of behaviors from this particular parenting style might also include:

• Monitoring the curriculum of the teacher to ensure that their children are on track with state benchmarks.
• Being critical of the school curriculum that it may not weigh enough to get into some of the top universities in the country, or possibly the world
• Never being satisfied with their children's work. Even when their children get As, they may look for ways to further motivate them.
• Involving their children in numerous activities outside of school so that they are well-rounded.
• Imposing many demands on their children to mimic the rigors and respon-sibilities of successful people.

Possible Reasoning

These parents differ from *investment parents* in that their motivations for their children stem from their desire to have their children succeed; they do not wish to live vicariously through their children's lives. They value hard work and independence, and see their role as guides in helping their children remain focused in their development. They are motivated by success and expect their children to always put forth 100% effort in everything that they do. They realize that no one will push their children harder than they will and take the responsibility of being a parent very seriously.

As Chua reveals in her book, much of this style is incorporated into certain cultures but in America today, many parents have adopted this style because it focuses on achievement through hard work and excellence. Some of them see that the path to success is to never to settle for mediocrity, and they can be the harshest critics of their children. They spend a considerable amount of time researching best practices for learning and mapping out the most efficient ways of getting into the best college and universities.

Teachers might often hear the following things from these parents:

- "I'm sorry. That might be good enough for the other students, but not for us."
- "He could do better; I know it."
- "We don't allow such things in our house."
- "I expected him to be covering much more material in your class."
- "May I see your assignments for the month? I like to have my children complete them ahead of time."

How Educators Could Best Work with These Parents

Children from these families are usually the high-achieving students who tend to excel in most of their classes. These parents are constantly motivating their children to excel and do not settle for average results. They will push their children, and in some cases even the teachers, if they feel that their children aren't being sufficiently challenged in their studies or extracurricular activities.

When used excessively, children can sometimes develop anxiety, low self-esteem, and depression from these types of environments. Frequent parent conferences may be necessary as well as differentiating their instruction to allow for advanced students or others who would like to extend their learning. Teachers will often have to implement differentiation in class that may have high-performing students in order to keep them focused and on track. One suggestion for these students is for them to create and maintain a portfolio based on the career they are most likely to pursue.

A teacher might also:

- Try not to give too much information that isn't pertinent to the current topic of the conference.
- Don't be afraid to ask administrators to attend a meeting if you feel it is necessary. Sometimes these parents can be very demanding, and only experienced teachers will be able to satisfactorily determine what a parent's responsibility is and what a teacher's responsibility is.
- Reflect on prior conversations and be careful what you say. These parents tend to remember every word and will reference it when needed.
- Be prepared for the parent meeting and make sure that you have all records and information that you think you will need.

VOLCANO PARENTS

Background

These parents are similar to *investment parents* in that both groups tend to feel that they have to address real or perceived limitations in their children. They differ in that *volcano parents* have the potential to "erupt" at any time, which of course poses some obvious problems for teachers and other professionals who work with these families (Elmore, 2011). In some cases, the goals of the parents are obvious but in other cases they may not be as evident. It is because of this reason that these eruptions can occur and may not have any indication that something is about to occur.

Perhaps every *hyper-parent* can potentially become a *volcano parent* depending on the circumstances, but when their confrontational ways become the norm for their interactions, it negatively impacts the parent-teacher relationship. These parents may also teeter on the edge of explosion and create tensions wherever they are. At other times, these parents may appear kind and mild-mannered, making their explosions all the more surprising.

They may also be described as:

- Confrontational
- Volatile
- Difficult
- Uncooperative

Examples

I have encountered a few *volcano parents* in my experience in the school system, and each situation was riddled with unbelievable tension. While working as a teacher, I once encountered a time in which one of my students no longer qualified for the upcoming basketball season because he had failed my class. I had discussed this with the student several times before grades were posted and warned him of the consequences if he failed my class for the marking period. I had been in constant contact with the mother, briefing her periodically about the lack of her son's progress in my class. She was very supportive and encouraged her son to stay focused on his studies, but much to both of our dismay, the student continued to slack off. I had met the father on several occasions and found him to have a very serious nature but was never presented with any problems. I was surprised to see the father show up in school to meet me one day to discuss his son's grades.

This was first time I felt completely blindsided at a parent meeting. I will never forget the complete anger and rage the father expressed to me at that meeting, where he placed the entire blame on me. I looked over to his wife to see if she would come to my aid and explain that I had kept them informed as was my professional responsibility, but unfortunately that didn't happen.

Some additional examples of behaviors from this particular parenting style might also include:

- Argumentative with educators
- Actions that ban them from certain events
- Explosively reacting to situations with total disregard for authority of their children's feelings
- Ability to immediately turn emotions

Possible Reasoning

These parents obviously have some anger issues that most often extend way beyond their interactions with classroom teachers. Their emotions, though, may intensify when it comes to dealing with their children because it is such a sensitive issue for them. It should be of no surprise that they most often have a history of violent reactions and negative experiences with school personnel. In other cases, their anger may be dormant for several years before it erupts.

It is possible that these parents are unaware of their inner anger issues and do not acknowledge the things that ignite their behaviors. They may even express regret and remorse after their eruptions but cannot always ensure that they will not happen again in the future.

Teachers might often hear the following things from these parents:

- "You have no right to talk to my child that way!"
- "I don't care what the school thinks, we're the parents!"
- "I will have my attorney look into this."
- "You are trying to ruin my child!"

How Educators Could Best Work with These Parents

Parents who employ this style usually have their reputations precede them and the word usually spreads about their explosions. What can be deceptive is that they may lie dormant for years without an outburst occurring. In some ways because of their reputation, teachers may be a little more careful with their dealings with *volcano parents*.

Teachers who have students of *volcano parents* must make sure that their safety remains their first priority. Teachers are recommended to see if they can clearly identify what the goals are and try to break them down into smaller goals with the parents so that they feel that they are part of the team.

Often in these conversations, parents may begin to realize that their children may not be equipped for the challenges that they have presented them with.

A teacher might also:

- Be proactive. Try to contact these parents before a problem arises or immediately when it does occur. Even though there is a potential that they might explode, it is best to remember that what the student did, or didn't do, was the reason for the phone call.
- Make sure the conferences are always professional and stick to the issue at hand, whatever it may be.
- Be sensitive and listen carefully, critically, and reflectively to parent concerns and complaints. What might start out as sounding like a complaint may turn into a plea for help.
- Keep good student records that include homework, phone and parent contacts, class participation tests grades, and performance, as well as how well their child is performing in relationship to the rest of the class or classes.
- Decide the location of the meeting yourself. A school media center or library where there is some privacy and other people around is a better location than an isolated classroom.
- Ask a colleague who also has the student or may have had him or her previously to attend the meeting with you.

Chapter Five

Hypo-Parenting

Hypo-parents tend to do less than what is usually expected of the average parent when it comes to guidance and supervision. The parents in this category are all similar in that their overall approach to parenting is characterized by being a much more laissez-faire view of raising children. These parents don't get overly involved in their children's lives and hardly stress about the responsibilities associated with parenting. They seemingly care for their children but do so in way that appears very different than what is expected. They do not feel the need to be overpowering or dominating their children's lives.

As with *hyper-parenting*, this style really only becomes an issue of concern when it becomes excessive, or when they are hands off to the point that there is little to no supervision in the home.

The general philosophy of these parents is that they tend to view parenting as a more relaxed and natural responsibility that does not need to have excessive rules and regulations for the children to follow. Rules, they feel, are much better when created by the children themselves when they are given the freedom to develop their own boundaries through their experiences in the world. In fact, many of these parents feel that allowing their children the freedom to set their own boundaries better prepares them for the future as adults when they are free to do as they wish.

They might also be exhibit additional behaviors such as being:

- Overly relaxed
- Not easily stressed
- Limited in the involvement in the minutia of parenting
- Encouraging of independence

If done with basic common sense, the right circumstances, and parents who know when intervene, this style can be very successful. In my own professional experience, I have encountered some products of *hypo-parenting* who have done very well in school, provided they had some structure of a supportive family. In far too many cases, my experience at the high school level has shown me that without some modicum of rules and boundaries that are set by attentive parents, these children have some difficulty guiding through adolescence all on their own.

For some of the students I have interacted with over the last twenty years, school is the only place of order and consistency in their lives. It, too, may also be the only place in which they have to be accountable. I have had the unfortunate experience of the extreme cases where students who do not have to follow any rules at home have a difficult time succeeding in school because they cannot conform to the structure and rigor of an educational setting. When children spend most of their lives in an environment where they construct their own rules, they react negatively to restrictions and protocol that serves to be the basis of most schools.

THE DISMISSIVE PARENT

Background

The *dismissive parent* tends to avoid, or dismiss, their children either physically or emotionally (Gottman and Declaire, 1998). They downplay the importance of these needs and provide limited attentiveness needed to raise a child. They may be unresponsive to the needs of their children and will often be viewed by others as cold and distant or just not responsible.

I would not necessarily describe these parents as adopting this style but rather that this style is an extension of their own lax personality. In most of my experiences, I have found these parents to be cold and distant in almost all of their relationships—seemingly detached from not only their children but their lives as well. Unlike *hyper-parents* who over-involve themselves in their children's affairs, *dismissive parents* tend to minimalize the importance of raising a child and put forth little effort in doing so. In some situations, they may have others, like tutors or nannies, attend to some of the responsibilities but in other cases the responsibilities may go unaddressed.

These parents are often viewed as:

- Dismissive
- Limited emotionally
- Aloof
- Detached
- Logical

Examples

These parents do not get overly excited or upset over most things, especially when it comes to their children. They tend to marginalize problems and challenges that occur in their own lives and use this same philosophy when it comes to raising their children. They often view good news in the same unemotional manner they do bad news, and it is usually quite difficult to truly understand and communicate with them.

These parents will minimally monitor their children's progress and will provide many financial obligations but little else. For example, if a *dismissive parent*'s child spends the night at a friend's house, the *dismissive parent*, much to the surprise of the mother hosting the sleepover, will not call or even follow-up to see if his or her child is okay.

Some other examples of their behavior might be:

- Will not show up to parent conferences even when requested to do so because of its importance
- Will not always return phone calls or emails in a timely fashion even when they know that it is an urgent matter
- Will schedule their vacations during the school year regardless of exams or other major events that are occurring
- May not show up to plays, performances, and other programs to support their children

Possible Reasoning

Most often these parents, who already may tend to be aloof and distant people, see things through a different lens then other parents. Their concept of love and warmth is much different than most others, and it is difficult to determine whether or not they are even capable of showing emotion. They are very analytical people who look at the world more practically and view things such as love and warmth as unnecessary frivolities.

I do not believe that these parents actively try to withhold their love from their children. In some instances, they may be unable to express it and will only provide superficial examples of attention.

Teachers might often hear the following things from these parents:

- "It's his life."
- "I don't see the big deal."
- "She has to learn sometime."
- "What do you want us to do about it?"

How Educators Could Best Work with These Parents

Children of *dismissive parents* may be affected in a number of ways. Most obviously, of course, would be that the students are quiet and withdrawn in response to the lack of affection given to them. As teachers, we are always drawn to these individuals and try our best to involve them in the classroom community through peer assistance, extra help, tutoring, or just good, old-fashioned TLC.

In some cases, these students enjoy interactions with their peers. In other cases, they sometimes follow the examples of their own parents. Teachers should make sure that these children are exposed to a variety of interactive activities in the classroom. In their later years, these children may begin to exhibit characteristics similar to their parents, such as being aloof. Encouraging participation in clubs and other activities should be emphasized as well as providing opportunities to explore self-expression.

A teacher might also:

- Require some kind of communication on a regular basis through phone, email, or other means to make sure that the parents are at least aware of what is happening in school.
- Create action plans for students when necessary that include specifics regarding timelines, follow-ups, and evaluation. These plans may also include activities that will help them be more social and communicative if necessary.
- View the parent as a fellow team member. Even suggesting things that they can do to be supportive at home could be a way of informing them that communication is important to a child's development, regardless of age.
- Don't generalize. Be specific. If there is a specific behavior that needs to be addressed, state it in clear terms and then provide an example of what you are getting at.

FREE RANGE PARENTING

Background

In the book *Free-Range Kids: How to Raise Safe, Self-Reliant Children (Without Going Nuts with Worry)*, the authors recommend giving children a great deal of space and freedom to explore and grow (Skenazy, 2009). It is explained that children who make most of their own decisions will learn through their choices what is best for them. This approach requires little training on the parent's part and is not meant to release parents from all of their parental responsibilities—although a great many of them are relinquished to the children.

This style, despite its name, actually requires a great deal of attention to be done correctly. Unfortunately, this isn't always the case in practice.

These parents will not impose a curfew and make it difficult for other parents because other children refer to them and ask their own parents to be more like them. Sometimes also referred to as the *Laissez-Faire Style*, these parents are only strict about their hands-off approach to parenting, which includes nearly every aspect of the child's life.

This style has often been criticized for being too lenient by many other parents. In some cases, *free range parents* may even be misrepresented as being negligent and not caring about their children at all. In many cases, this couldn't be farther from the truth. These parents prescribe to a different set of beliefs that celebrates independence and lack of forced rules in favor of a more natural, inquiry-based approach.

They might also be described as:

- Free-spirited
- Respectful of individual rights
- Critical of large organizations
- Not being concerned with what other people think of them
- Not imposing many rules
- Frowning on negative consequences
- Enforcing little if any punishment or discipline
- Being care-free

Examples

Lenore Skenazy, the author of the book *Free-Range Kids: How to Raise Safe, Self-Reliant Children (Without Going Nuts with Worry),* has been criticized for allowing her nine-year-old child to ride the New York City subway system by herself. The author responded with how allowing children to make decisions for themselves had been going on for a long time in previous generations and it was only now that we have been restricting these freedoms that had been prevalent. What appears like irresponsible parenting by many is viewed by the *free range parent* as an opportunity to allow children to assume responsibility at an early age.

These parents can also be found allowing their children to play and explore with little supervision. In some cases, this forms very mature and independent children; in other cases, these children grow up having little idea of limitations and boundaries that are extremely important in their formative years. Lately, though, *free range parents* have received a great deal of criticism for their lenient ways by allowing their children too much freedom at earlier ages.

Some additional examples of behaviors from this particular parenting style might also include:

- They don't impose a curfew and allow their children to stay out as late as they want.
- They might impose few, if any, restrictions on junk food and other sugary snacks.
- *Free range parents* will provide limited supervision of their children. At parties, they are the parents who never get up to check on their kids.
- They tend not to involve themselves in their children's affairs unless invited or specifically instructed to do so.
- They will overlook or not address bad behavior, nor will they acknowledge good behavior.

Possible Reasoning

These parents can be put into one of two categories. They have either made a conscious decision to allow their children to explore the world and believe that through their exploration they will begin to eventually impose their own boundaries, or they are oblivious to parenting responsibilities and provide the most basic supervision of their children.

In either case, they are not strict rule makers and do not subscribe to any real philosophy other than live and let live. They feel that by not providing too many rules, children will grow up and make better decisions. *Free range parents* believe that this independent, inquiry-based approach is much more natural and allows the child to develop at his or her own rate, which will help them be much happier and healthier adults.

Teachers might often hear the following things from these parents:

- "We don't like to put too many restrictions on our children."
- "She does things her own way."
- "We're not very strict at home."
- "We like to have him make his own decisions about what happens in his school responsibilities."
- "Is this something we really have to come in for? Can't we just discuss it on the phone?"

How Educators Could Best Work with These Parents

Despite the criticisms that exist with this particular approach, I have witnessed this style work very effectively on many occasions, with the right child as well as the right circumstances. In the cases that this was most effective, the children were from socioeconomic backgrounds that allowed for more freedom and exploration. In addition, these families also provided the resources needed to address and rectify problems that occurred from the freedom that this style promoted. Most of these children were able to handle responsibility and made very good choices that were noticeably admirable.

Unfortunately, in other situations, the students did not fare as well as their counterparts. These students could be described as oppositional, defiant, disrespectful, and even dangerous. Because they were allowed the freedom to explore their boundaries, they demanded to be treated as an adult even if they didn't exhibit any characteristics of maturity. In most cases, these students will conflict with school authorities at almost every turn. In the best cases, these students, who have found their own boundaries, are able to succeed because they tend to be more mature than many of their peers.

Meetings with these parents can sometimes prove to be very frustrating because there is very little reinforcement being done at home. Therefore, if a student is struggling in a class, little support will be able to be provided by the parents besides verbal encouragement because they tend to frown on negative consequences.

A teacher might also:

- Try to use language that addresses the student's specific behavior and not something that can be interpreted as critiquing the parent or over-criticizing the student.
- Find ways (newsletters, email, website, etc.) that provide information for parents and keep them updated with what is going on in the classroom. Having parents respond to emails and such makes them more accountable.
- Provide clear and concise plans for addressing academic and/or behavioral issues that include an action plan with timetables, follow-ups, and evaluations. Make sure that a parental component is included. Even if only basic compliance is performed, that is better than nothing at all.

THE BEST FRIEND PARENT

Background

As the name most obviously implies, in this family dynamic, parents view their children as friends who are equal to them in most every regard. These parents do very little in the way of disciplining their children and in some instances actually encourage much of their negative behavior. *Best friend parents* tend to like many of the same things as their children, such as fashion and music. They are often even described by other children as the "cool parent" (Hellmich, 2004).

Although there are rules in the house, the decision making as to what is permissible is far from the majority of families. In some ways, these parents take on a "dorm like" existence in their house. They interact with their children in a friendship capacity and provide an environment free from most rules and restrictions even beginning at an early age.

They might also be described as:

- Immature
- Very concerned with staying relevant
- Attentive to their children's interests
- Good listeners with their children
- Look and act much younger than their actual age

Examples

Best friend parents engage in behaviors that still surprise me even today. They most often range from harmless and often embarrassing to potentially dangerous.

The former group might exhibit such behaviors as being lenient and having long talks with their children to convince them of doing the right things. This group could also be found engaging in some activities geared toward the younger generation such as dressing like a teenager or getting tattoos that are in style.

The latter group might engage in such things as buying beer for their children's prom weekend, knowingly permitting drugs, and allowing their co-ed sleepovers with little supervision. In some cases, they may rationalize their actions by insisting that they are providing a safe environment that addresses the issue of under-age drinking in a much more pragmatic manner.

Best friend parents will often promote a kind of philosophy that seems to justify their actions. They also tend to be the ones that dress in the current fashion of the youth of the day. They not only allow their children to get tattoos but also get one with them as a sort of bonding experience. Children love these parents until there is disagreement where the parent is forced to enact some sort of discipline. By that time, they have already lost the role of the parent and are not respected.

Some additional examples of behaviors from this particular parenting style might also include:

- Parents having conversations about topics that would not be considered inappropriate between adults and children, and would more closely resemble adult conversations
- Permitting children to make decisions beyond their maturity level just because they don't want to be "un-cool"

- Engaging in immature and potentially dangerous behaviors with their children that may be unethical, illegal, or just plain inappropriate
- Imposing few rules and encouraging their children's friends to engage in their permissive lifestyle

Possible Reasoning

In most cases, these parents see the world as overwrought with rules and regulations. They have come to realize the importance of allowing children to be able to be free is of much more concern to them than following a bunch of do's and do not's.

Best friend parents may not feel equipped to manage the many responsibilities of being a parent. They may also believe that parenting is much more than exerting authority over children and more about the bonds that they develop. In any event, in these families the boundaries can sometimes be indistinct and very vague.

As one might suppose, this can pose potential problems later in life, especially during adolescence. They may feel that the friendships they have with their children are much more rewarding than what they would experience if they assumed traditional parenting techniques. They have come to terms with the possibility that being a friend will last much longer than being a parent.

Teachers might often hear the following things from these parents:

- "I know him better than even his own friends."
- "I like to stay current with what the kids are into these days."
- "I'm not one of those old fuddy-duddy parents."
- "I'm not blind to what's happening in society today."
- "I'm my kid's best friend."

How Educators Could Best Work with These Parents

These types of students can pose some unique challenges to teachers due to the lack of rules at home. Because they are not strict disciplinarians, it can make classroom management sometimes difficult for the teacher to establish and reinforce. In certain circumstances, these parents will even defend their children's bad behavior by dismissing it or not addressing it. This seldom does little to prevent it from reoccurring again.

Teachers are encouraged to establish clear rules and consequences early in the year so that parents are aware of their children's expectations as well as their own. It is important that these parents never misconstrue teachers' rules as an extension of their own parenting skills. They are much more supportive when they view the teachers' rules and expectations as a connection to instruction and the curriculum that occurs within the school.

A teacher might also:

- Keep good student records that include homework, phone and parent contacts, class participation tests grades, and performance, as well as how well their child is performing in relationship to the rest of the class or classes. It is important for these parents to see how their children are progressing in relationship to others their age.
- In meeting with these parents, make sure to have a sufficient amount of examples and evidence to support what you want to share with them. In certain cases, they can be convinced that their children may need help in a specific area and will address it the best way they see fit.
- Don't be afraid to ask administrators to attend a meeting if you feel it is necessary. *Best friend parents* can be frustrating at times, both for newer teachers as well as veterans who still maintain an idea of traditional parents properly disciplining their children.
- Know when to ask for an outside perspective such as a veteran teacher, a supervisor, or an administrator. Sometimes, teachers can get so involved with student affairs that they may lose objectivity. Bringing in an outside perspective can help a teacher regain objectivity.

IDLE PARENTING

Background

In his book, *The Idle Parent: Why Laid-Back Parents Raise Happier and Healthier Kids*, the author Tom Hodgkinson highlights a more modest approach to parenting that does not involve all of the bells and whistles that some other approaches recommend (2010). The author instead suggests that parents live in the present and not be so concerned about planning for the future. Hodgkinson writes that sometimes parents become so overly concerned with preparing their children for their futures they miss out on opportunities for happiness in the present.

Idle parents are not overly concerned with many of the things most struggle with (e.g., grades, college, and social status are all things that will somehow figure themselves out). They take the opportunity to deal with the problems and challenges of the day as it occurs.

They might also be described as:

- Living in the moment
- Vicarious
- Sensible

- Focused
- Not easily stressed
- Selfish

Examples

Idle parents do not see the need to worry about the ramifications of their actions, knowing that they will deal with any consequences as they occur. For example, they will go away on long vacations during the school year, either taking their children with them or leaving them in the safety of trusted relatives, because it works for their schedule. They will not examine the repercussions of their children missing out on tests and projects but only view a problem that needs an immediate solution.

They also value their children's time alone as much as they value their own adult time and set clear boundaries with their children regarding them. They believe in the importance of their own interests and personal development as much as they do their children's and encourage them to become responsible adults. When done correctly, this approach can be categorized as *balanced parenting*, but if it becomes extreme then it becomes *idle parenting*.

Some additional examples of behaviors from this particular parenting style might also include the following:

- They may miss important school deadlines and automatically expect to have extensions.
- They do not understand the importance of projects being turned in on time and will expect their children to be granted additional time to turn things in another day.
- *Idle parents* will not get involved in disputing a teacher's discipline. They understand that the school has rules and although they may not believe in them, they usually will not contest them.
- They are not always considerate of other people's schedules. They are not necessarily rude but can be so immersed in their own lives that they cannot understand others.

Possible Reasoning

These parents tend to promote a carpe diem philosophy toward life that greatly influences their parenting techniques. They look at the grand scheme of the universe and realize that some of the smaller things, especially those that occur in school, are really insignificant. This philosophy was perhaps never more prevalent than during the *Me Generation* of the 1970s where parents felt the need to do their own thing while trying to balance the responsibilities of parenting as they searched to discover themselves. *Idle parents* are generally mild-mannered and prefer to give people their space.

Teachers might often hear the following things from these parents:

- "There are things more important than school."
- "We have our lives as well"
- "She will have to learn that on her own."
- "Alone time is important."
- "That's just not that important to us."

How Educators Could Best Work with These Parents

Educators will notice that these students can have the tendency to be lost through the cracks if they are not carefully monitored. Because the parents do not always remain consistently focused on their children's progress in school, there is a possibility that certain deficits or problems could occur without them realizing it. This, of course, makes teachers' jobs very difficult because they have to be very cognizant of all of their students to ensure that none fall through the cracks.

Teachers may need to try several times in reaching out to these parents. In some cases, they can have success with increased participation. For example, in the lower grades, and perhaps in the higher ones as well, teachers can provide minimum parental expectations in the beginning of the school year. This can include activities such as parent interviews, video projects, etc.— anything that will get the parents involved in their children's academics.

A teacher might also:

- Create specific action plans for students when necessary and have the parents provide input.
- Maintain the mantra that this parent loves his or her child. Sometimes this can be difficult because teachers feel like parents should be devoting more time to the care and supervision of their children's progress. It is important to remember that some families can be masking even greater pain behind their aloofness. Teachers must probe carefully because sometimes in the midst of trying to find answers we get them and then the real challenges begin. And if you're not willing to go the distance, tread lightly.
- Take notes during parent meetings to document what was said. Later on, these words may be needed to remind the parents of what was discussed.
- Have a specific set of things you are willing to offer the parents and make sure to follow-up (i.e., extra help, additional assignments, make-up work, daily or weekly contacts, etc.).

KARAOKE PARENTS

Background

Karaoke parents get their name from the uninhibitedness of the participant singers known to frequent the karaoke bars (Elmore, 2011). Although there are similarities to the *best friend parents*, these parents differ in that they are more concerned with being liked than appearing young and hip.

They may wish to be friends with their children, but feel that to be liked is much more of an important characteristic. Much like their counterparts, they don't establish clear parameters that help their children establish norms and boundaries but prefer the attention they attain socially from their actions. Their overwhelming desire to be viewed as a great parent usually forces them to give in to their children's demands and prevents them from demonstrating authority or discipline when necessary. Whereas *best friend parents* want to impress their children and their friends, *karaoke parents* wish to impress the other adults, including teachers, with how great they are.

They might also be described as:

- Self-indulgent
- Insecure
- Extroverted
- Easily offended
- Self-centered

Examples

Karaoke parents will devote their time to showing up to the right events and participating in the high-profile activities that will bring them the most accolades from others. They engage in semi-permissive parenting that imposes the fewest amounts of rules while still appearing like a model parent. They will stage elaborate parties and purchase expensive gifts so that they receive the praise that they desire.

Karaoke parents will go to great lengths to keep up appearances. This often can be done by coaxing their children to do things by offering gifts and other rewards. They differ from other parents who use a reward system for positive reinforcement because they use it almost exclusively as their only parenting strategy. In addition, it is their concern of how they will appear to others that separates them distinctly from other styles.

Some additional examples of behaviors from this particular parenting style might also include the following:

- Will host elaborate sleepover parties that are action-packed and attempt to set the highest bar of their circle of friends
- Will purchase the most expensive gifts for their children so that they receive attention from their children's peers as well as other parents.
- Are extraordinarily nice and accommodating to their children's friends, lavishing them with gifts and kind words
- Will engage in elaborate events for their children but also try to share the spotlight with them

Possible Reasoning

These parents may feel that their actions are justified because they always benefit their children. The *karaoke parents* that I have worked with in my career most often appear to be seeking recognition. In certain cases, they can be more refined and less obvious. In others, they appear gratuitous and desperate. There was never a time I didn't feel that these parents cared deeply about their children, but I always felt that their desire to be acknowledged for their parental prowess was much more important to them. In some ways, it seems that *karaoke parents* want to buy their way to a child's heart. Surprisingly, in some cases I have actually seen it work.

Teachers might often hear the following things from these parents:

- "I know what it's like to be young."
- "I care what my kid thinks of me."
- "I trust my daughter; she's mature."
- "I know it's expensive but he deserves it."

How Educators Could Best Work with These Parents

Teachers sometimes have difficulties with students who are used to being given everything they want. Because of this, they can sometimes become very obstinate when they don't get their way and can create problems in the classroom. These students need honest and constructive criticism from their teachers. In order for this to be most effective, a productive learning environment must be established where students are encouraged to take risks and explore interests in which they may not easily excel. Clear classroom rules and procedures that are fair and consistent will help in addressing these types of students.

A teacher might also:

- View the parent as a fellow team member. Assign the parent different tasks at supporting what occurs in the classroom and periodically follow-up on how well those tasks are being executed.

- Acknowledge true accomplishments in which students push themselves to go beyond what they thought they could do.
- Provide examples of student work to clearly illustrate expectations of excellence.
- Encourage students to enter local, state, regional, and national contests to expose themselves to competition that exists beyond the classroom as well as the school.

LAID-BACK MOM/DAD

Background

This type of parent doesn't get upset or overly involved in their child's successes nor failures—as a matter of fact, they very seldom get upset at all. They differ from the *free range* and *idle parents* in that there is not a conscious decision to not impose boundaries as much as there is a lack of emphasis placed on it. They do not stress themselves with addressing the disciplinary, academic, or behavioral issues with their children and are not easily excitable or terribly motivated. These parents tend to be low energy and distribute the same ambivalence to their child's A on a test as they do with an F (Sotonoff, 2011). They are usually pretty even tempered in most aspects of their life and will confront most of the challenges of raising their children with a laid-back philosophy. When disciplining their children, their punishments are usually very mild and rarely ever do anything to discourage that behavior again.

They might also be described as:

- Calm
- Sensitive
- Easy going
- Very lenient

Examples

Children of *laid-back parents* usually exhibit similar characteristics in that they tend not to be overly concerned about most things and will approach challenges on their own terms. This means that they may shrug things off or hold them off to address at a later time.

In many cases, they can be very charming and popular children, because of their free spirit approach toward life, but may also not take things seriously, especially school work. These parents will not be overly involved in the academic progress of their children. They are more concerned that their children are content with their lives and the decisions they make.

Laid-back parents are considered by their children's friends as the cool parents who don't impose curfews and provide an environment where anything goes. They turn their heads to anything and never get overly involved in their children's affairs.

Some additional examples of behaviors from this particular parenting style might also include the following:

- They might be the last parents to turn in permission slips.
- They do not plan for things.
- They might not respond to teacher requests.
- They might not engage in discipline.

Possible Reasoning

These parents usually have a philosophy that permeates everything in their life, including child rearing. They tend to find everyday living far too stressful and have taken a philosophy of not letting the small things worry them. They approach each challenge in much the same way: calmly and with minimal talking and few actions.

In most cases, this approach is more an extension of the parent's own personality than it is a philosophy that has been consciously developed, although I'm sure it can be conscious in some instances. *Laid-back parents* can also be carrying on the tradition from their like-minded parents who could have played an influential role in how they were raised themselves.

Teachers might often hear the following things from these parents:

- "We can't make him do what he doesn't want to do. We would rather he make his own decisions."
- "We don't like to impose too many rules at our house. That's just not our way."
- "Let's just see what happens. There's no harm in that."
- "She's a great kid, and we just don't like to hassle her too much about these things."
- "We don't like to get too involved in these things."

How Educators Could Best Work with These Parents

As educators, conversations with these parents can sometimes prove to be very frustrating, especially when it comes to conversations that happen to be about student achievement. Despite advice and urging from others, these parents tend to continue having marginal involvement in their children's lives. Teachers must still try to continue providing feedback and communication to these parents, trying a variety of ways that include email, phone calls, or even letters.

Children of *laid-back parents* can sometimes continue the tradition of low expectations in the classroom. Teachers are encouraged to engage students to maximize their potential and create assignments that require children to redo, improve, or edit projects that also include self-evaluation and reflection.

This style can sometimes also create situations where children are less likely to see their parents as authority figures (Leon, 2013). Sometimes, these perceptions can find their ways into the school where some of the children of *laid-back parents* feel the same way about the teachers and other professionals as well. By providing clear expectations and boundaries, teachers can model to these students that respect is an important attribute.

A teacher might also:

- Find ways (newsletters, email, website, etc.) that provide information for parents and keep them updated with what is going on in the classroom.
- Try not to generalize. Do not say, "He doesn't do any homework" when you can say, "He has not completed fifteen of the possible twenty homework assignments."
- Maintain the mantra that this parent loves his or her child. Even though the parent may not exhibit the characteristics that you realize would be more effective for a student's academic progress, there are a multitude of variables that make up a family dynamic that are beyond your control.
- Give it 100%. At the end of the day, regardless of how many more successes we think we could have gotten with our students, we must feel that we gave it everything we had. Try to help change the things that you can for the positive and realize that some things may be beyond your control.

PUSSY CAT PARENTING

Background

Pussy cat parents are known for their soft touch in raising their children. They are very aware of their children's sensitivities and address issues carefully so as not to upset them (Strauss, 2011). They are not necessarily afraid of their children, but they prefer being gentle with them because they do not want to press too hard and create further emotional distress. They are overly attentive and are concerned that most other parents aren't as sensitive as they should be regarding how their children feel. They place a significant amount of importance on the emotional and psychological well-being of children as the key to a happy and successful life.

In some cases, ironically, these adults might not be as sensitive with other children or other adults in their lives. The relationship they have with their children may be exclusive where they surprisingly see very little value in treating others with the same level of tender care they use with their children. Their skills lie with their own children, and they pride themselves on being very attentive parents who are better at communicating with their children because of these close ties that have been formed.

They might also be described as:

• Overly sensitive
• Attentive
• Believe they know their children better than anyone else
• Fearful of confrontations
• Tend to lose perspective in situations involving their children

Examples

These parents will downplay any misbehavior from their children and deflect any criticism that involves them. In defending their own children, they may put down or demean other children, arguing that their behaviors are far worse than that of their own children. They will make excuses for their actions as well as their children's and always find an explanation to justify what they do. If they ever happen to discipline their children, punishments are usually very light and superficially address the real issue.

I once encountered parents who, although their daughter was involved in a very serious fight with another girl who had to be hospitalized, downplayed the entire incident. At times in the conversation, the mother even said, without an ounce of pity in her voice, that the other girl had it coming to her. To my knowledge, this mother never imposed any of her own discipline and continuously fought the court systems because she felt that her daughter's actions were completely justified.

Some additional examples of behaviors from this particular parenting style might also include the following:

• Will take orders from their children
• Will not support discipline of any kind
• Take their children's side of a situation as the only side
• Always will be afraid of hurting their children's feelings
• Will not get involved in school matters unless it is to get their children reduced sentences

Possible Reasoning

These parents are usually meek, fear confrontations, and do not like to engage in any form of debate when interacting with their children. They may interact with others in much the same way, but this is not always the case. In the latter, this is usually indicative that this is much more of the parent's mild and passive personality than it has to do with their conscious decision to parent in this fashion.

They tend to be less demonstrative parents who try desperately to please their children. In some cases, they may be more sensitive to their emotions because they know firsthand how it feels when parents don't take their children's emotions into consideration.

Teachers might often hear the following things from these parents:

- "I don't have to discipline my son. He already knows right from wrong."
- "I think you were too hard on her. She is very sensitive."
- "I would rather you tell him."
- "He's just a kid."
- "We're not overly strict parents."
- "We deal with her in our own way."

How Educators Could Best Work with These Parents

These parents will always feel that any form of criticism or discipline by a teacher is excessive. These children can pose some challenges within the class because they are used to being dealt with in a very delicate way and may react violently or withdraw if a teacher is too hard with his or her criticism. In either event, these students may be very sensitive when criticized for their actions. Teachers usually realize very early in the school year which students are more sensitive than the others, and teachers can address these students accordingly to prevent them from creating any anxiety. Creating activities and projects that help build self-confidence with students can greatly benefit their overall development.

A teacher might also:

- Create action plans for students when necessary.
- Have a clear set of classroom rules complete with consequences that is shared with all students and parents in the beginning of the year.
- Provide opportunities to reflect on projects and assignments so that they can see how much they are progressing.
- Help students, as well as parents, understand the value and importance of constructive criticism and how it fits into progress and success in all areas of life.
- Reflect on prior conversations and be careful what you say. These parents tend to remember every word and will reference it when needed.

WISHBONE PARENTING

Background

This style is named after the tradition of making a wish when pulling apart a bone at holiday dinners (Bean, 2010). This approach allows for constant struggles with the child resulting in the parents wishing for their situations to get better (Belkin, 2012). There is a genuine desire in trying to improve things for their children but the lack of follow-through prevents any chance of improving things. These parents want the best for their children but lack the self-discipline and experience to be able to remain consistent with their parenting approach. Instead of working at trying to implement some sort of interventions, they hope for things to change and do very little in trying to create any substantial changes themselves.

They might also be described as:

- Meek
- Optimistic
- Easily frustrated
- Nonjudgmental

Examples

Unlike some of the previously discussed styles, these parents might impose disciplinary actions on their children but because there is a lack of consistency, will not be as effective as a style that adheres to imparting consistent consequences. They might make these declarations in public but due to a variety of reasons they are either unable or unwilling to fully execute what they say they are going to do. Children are very adept at understanding this kind of situation and will sometimes take the chance of disobeying because they know that a punishment is not always assured nor accompanied. *Wishbone parents* will discuss their plight with others and always look for advice on how to improve their situation.

Some additional examples of behaviors from this particular parenting style might also include:

- Complaining about their situations but not doing much to change it
- Asking for advice but never putting it into action
- Getting frustrated at their present situation
- Blaming others for the problems they are facing
- Verbalizing their hopes in front of others

Possible Reasoning

These parents wish for change but lack the means, resources, or motivation to follow-through with any one particular approach and instead look toward hoping for a miracle to occur. In some cases, a miracle does happen, but in far too many cases, children realize that their parents are impatient and will use that against them. Unfortunately, wishing for good things to happen does not guarantee success in raising children. I have witnessed that in almost all cases throughout my career that turning a blind eye to issues never is a good idea. It is hard to determine if *wishbone parents* lack the energy that it takes to make changes in their lives or whether they make excuses that prevents them from changing.

Teachers might often hear the following things from these parents:

- "I tried that already with her, but it just doesn't work."
- "I don't know what to do."
- "I just hope for things to get better for us."
- "I've tried everything but nothing seems to work with him."
- "What do you suggest?"

How Educators Could Best Work with These Parents

For the parents who find change impossible, this could pose some serious challenges to the classroom teacher. Educators are advised to model consistency in the classroom so that students will be able to practice consistency themselves. These parents will most often look for advice from educational professionals, so it is always advisable that teachers be aware of local parenting groups they can be referred to.

A teacher might also:

- Provide best practices regarding strategies for addressing behaviors
- Provide age milestones that can be used as goals for parenting
- Create action plans for students when necessary
- Be firm, fair, and consistent
- Have a specific set of things you are willing to offer the parents (i.e., extra help, additional assignments, make-up work, daily or weekly contacts, etc.)

Chapter Six

Traditional/Neo-traditional

The *traditional/neo-traditional* style is characterized by a return to a more traditional view of parenting that often includes a two-parent household with one parent providing the primary economic resources and the other assuming the care for child rearing. In 1950s America, this most often saw the father assuming the role of the financial provider while the mother traditionally stayed home and tended to the children and the house. Ideally, there would be a shared responsibility with all of these tasks, but not in all cases was this true. This type of family configuration was the archetype for well over four hundred years. Not until the 1970s did the increase in divorce and one-parent household begin to shift the national landscape.

Although they may look different today, the basic structure of one parent at work and one staying at home, or where the parents try their very best to maintain a work schedule where one parent is available at all times, is the basis for *traditional/neo-traditional parenting*.

Today, *traditional/neo-traditional parents* may assume a variety of configurations, such as, but not limited to, the following:

- The father goes to work and the mother assumes a majority of the responsibility of caring for the children.
- The mother goes to work and the father assumes a majority of the responsibility of caring for the children.
- The mother goes to work and the other mother assumes a majority of the responsibility of caring for the children.
- The father goes to work and the other father assumes a majority of the responsibility of caring for the children.

This can include transgender parents, blended families, and extended relatives, such as grandparents or siblings, who are raising a family. Although they may look different from *Leave It to Beaver* and other shows from the so-called Golden Age, they retain the basic structure of a division of labor and emphasize their philosophy of the importance of one parent keeping an eye on the children.

These parents are generally perceived as:

- Patient
- Easy to talk to
- Willing to donate their time
- Flexible
- Attentive

ACTIVE PARENTING

Background

The concept of *active parenting* is partially based upon the work of Alfred Adler and Rudolf Dreikurs (Scheve, n.d.). *Active parents*, who tend to focus on behaviors, are most concerned about raising responsible children. This is a somewhat balanced approach for parents who try to stay abreast of new trends and integrate them in their parenting style. These parents are very different from the *book of the month parents* who never seem to find the right fit for their parenting approach. These parents differ in that they utilize some of the new research and trends that are available but don't allow that information to become an obstacle for them to achieve their focus in rearing their children. These parents tend to take a proactive approach and do not wait for problems to occur but will look to cut them off before they occur. *Active parents* are always looking for new research to assist them in the many new challenges that arise with the changing times.

They might also be described as:

- Proactive
- Thoughtful
- Self-assured
- Reliable
- Cooperative

Examples

Active parents are interested in character education and ensuring their children are raised with integrity. Although there is not one particular approach that they uniformly prescribe to, they are all similar in that they are constantly looking for the best practice for their families. These parents pride themselves on varying the approaches used from their respective childhoods and on looking to find new and more effective ways of child rearing. They fully engage themselves in the parenting process and seek to find new ways of helping their children mature.

Teaching of self-esteem is another important factor of *active parenting* that will be seen in many of their actions. These parents will utilize everyday activities as opportunities to teach about values or provide encouragement to their children. For example, seeing a neighbor who needs help, a parent can encourage the child to provide assistance. Each positive act is accompanied by verbal recognition and praise.

Some additional examples of behaviors from this particular parenting style might also include the following:

- Parents will join the parent-teacher association to be involved in school and community affairs and also be a role model for their children.
- *Active parents* will contact teachers when they see a change in child's behavior at home and ask for assistance and suggestions to address the issue cooperatively.
- These parents will seek out tutors as soon as their child's grades begin to slip. They do not blame the school first. They are more concerned with addressing the behavior than finding blame.
- They will work cooperatively with their children to plan for their futures after school.
- They will act upon teacher's recommendations.

Possible Reasoning

Active parents are goal directed who are very concerned with the moral and professional status of their children. These parents tend to want to try their best to make sure that their children are responsible and respectable children who will be able to successfully function in life. They value hard work and organization, and view these as critical to successful parenting. They try their best to model appropriate behavior and like to be hands-on with their children.

These parents may have had excellent role models in their own parents and are thus carrying on the tradition. In other cases, they may have just somehow figured along the way of their own lives how important parental guidance is in the happiness and well-being of a child. *Active parents* do not set unreal expectations for their children. Their philosophy is that they want their children to reach their full potential, whatever that may be. They clearly see their role is to help them and support them in accomplishing this goal.

Teachers might often hear the following things from these parents:

- "Do you have any suggestions about what I can do?"
- "How is my son doing in relation to the rest of the class?"
- "I tried that already. I think I might need to try something new."
- "I don't care how often I have to come in and make sure she's doing what she needs to do."
- "We support her in her decision of where she wants to go to college."

How Educators Could Best Work with These Parents

These parents appreciate frequent feedback and are not afraid of constructive criticism. In many cases, they tend to be the ones that will ask for advice and actually attempt to implement it. They are very concerned that their children grow up to understand the values of morality and sound judgment. They work well with teachers who share similar values as them but will respect teachers even when they do not.

Active parents like to feel that they are welcome in their children's schools. They like to be involved and look forward to talent shows and presentations where they can visit and support their children.

A teacher might also:

- Make sure to keep these parents in frequent contact.
- Create actions plans for students when necessary.
- Do not be afraid to professionally disagree with the *active parent*. These parents appreciate solid criticism and will act upon it if they feel it works for their child.
- Know the child's pertinent information. If the child has an IEP (Individualized Learning Plan) or accommodations with a 504 Plan, make sure that you are familiar with what is written in it and that you are in compliance.
- Keep these parents engaged and look for ways that they can participate in school functions.

AVAILABLE PARENTS

Background

John Duffy describes *available parents* as those who don't have the fear and apprehension that many parents have today. They are fully emotionally and physically available to their children at all times (2011). These parents focus on communicating with their children in a positive way and accept them for who they are. *Available parents* focus on their children's strengths and encourage them to be happy and well-adjusted children.

They accept their children for who they are and do not try to imprint an identity but rather encourage the development of their own individuality. They believe that forging strong relationships with their children is the key to good parenting. *Available parents* do not overly discipline their children, but they also don't shy away from it. They are moderate in the types and forms of punishments that they mete out to their children.

They might also be described as:

- Sensitive
- Nurturing
- Easy-going
- Mild-mannered
- Even-tempered

Examples

Available parents can often be found as members of the parent-teacher association, as class mothers, or as other types of volunteers. They do these things without any agenda of recognition for their children's advancement. They do these things only to be closer to their children.

Available parents work very hard at being part of their children's lives and experiencing things with them like attending athletic competitions, chaperoning trips, and volunteering at local groups with them. It matters little to them if their child is the starting pitcher or never even plays in the game; they continue to show their support regardless of whether their child is a starter or a bench warmer. They enjoy the quality time and try their hardest to maintain their participation with them well into their high school years.

Some additional examples of behaviors from this particular parenting style might include:

- Attending all sporting events and practices
- Being available to attend all conferences and meetings
- Understanding that part of being a parent is also being a good role model
- Understanding the value of volunteering and participating with their children in these activities
- Maintaining an active role in community or church programs

Possible Reasoning

These parents value spending time with their children and cherish the memories they create. They show a genuine appreciation in being able to be a parent and are dedicated to finding ways around their hectic schedules to remain prominent in their children's lives. They are able to find the right balance of professional, family, and personal responsibilities, and are role models for maturity. These parents are fueled by the desire to remain relevant to their children and their interests. They display few of their own unresolved issues that impact their parenting and are mostly average people.

Teachers might often hear the following things from these parents:

- "I enjoy being part of my child's life."
- "I don't mind giving up my time for my child."
- "I enjoy spending quality time with her."
- "We'll find the time to be there."

How Educators Could Best Work with These Parents

These parents can be very supportive and work well with teachers. They tend to like to participate in field trips and other school functions. They enjoy being involved and make themselves available to volunteer at a moment's notice.

Teachers are encouraged to maintain good communication with *available parents*, who value being involved with the school as it pertains to their children. They may become disappointed if they are marginalized and offered few opportunities to participate in school functions.

A teacher might also:

- Find ways (newsletters, email, website, etc.) that provide information for parents and keep them updated with what is going on in the classroom.
- Involve the parents in classroom field trips.
- Try not to promise something that might not be possible to deliver.
- Schedule regular student demonstrations showcasing talent and projects. These can be live or videoed and posted on a secure website.

BACKBONE PARENTING

Background

Despite many of the pressures of the modern family, these parents don't mind tackling the difficult problems with firm and consistent discipline of their children (Belkin, 2012). They are reminiscent of the old-fashioned type of parenting, having strong family values and insisting that their children maintain them. *Backbone parents* also realize that parenting means that their children will not always like what they do but realize that this friction is part of being a parent. They have clear lines between child and parent, and they set boundaries for their children and expect them to be respected. They can at times be very authoritarian, as explained by Baumrind (1967). Although they are strict, they are not necessarily open to different ideas and believe that the parents must be in control. They also try to instill in their children a sense of responsibility as they help them to become productive and well-adjusted adults.

They might also be described as:

- Assertive
- Demanding
- Strict
- Have the desire to be in control
- Responsive

Examples

Backbone parents aren't afraid to make tough decisions and are not concerned with how they may appear to teachers, other parents, or even their children. They fully understand that parenting is a difficult task and sometimes they may have to do things that their children will not like. These parents are active in their children's lives and establish clear boundaries that they expect to be followed.

For example, *backbone parents* might decide that after warning their daughter of the ramifications of not being able to attend a friend's birthday party, she still got in trouble in school. Where some parents might make concessions and change their mind, *backbone parents* will not relent and will stick to what they said.

Some additional examples of behaviors from this particular parenting style might also include the following:

- Don't mind when teachers call, even with bad news
- Will act on teacher recommendations
- Consistent with their discipline
- Judicious in how they mete out their punishments
- Will impose the discipline they say they are going to do

Possible Reasoning

Backbone parents are firm believers in rules and expect their children to follow those rules. They have a philosophy that they are responsible for instilling morality and values in their family. In some cases, this is because this style has been passed down from their own parents; in others, it is a new revelation. One study by Stephen Bahr of Brigham Young University in Utah even found that authoritative parents who closely supervise their children and provide support and encouragement are less likely to have adolescents engage in drinking alcohol (Wade, 2010).

Teachers might often hear the following things from these parents:

- "I will handle this."
- "I will talk to her when I get home."
- "She knows better than to act like this."
- "This won't happen again with him; I can guarantee it."
- "Call me immediately if she acts up in class again."

How Educators Could Best Work with These Parents

Because the parents tend to be strict rule followers themselves, they most often have productive interaction with teachers. These parents appreciate frequent feedback from teachers and do not mind receiving constructive criticism about their children. They like to be involved and work closely with the school to support their endeavors.

Backbone parents prefer face-to-face meetings but will use other forms of communication to monitor the progress of their children. They prefer to keep their children challenged and engaged, and will let teachers know if they do not think that this is occurring in the classroom.

A teacher might also:

- In meeting with these parents, make sure to have sufficient amounts of examples and evidence to support what you want to share with them.
- Be prepared for the parent meeting and make sure that you have all records and information that you think you will need.
- Provide parents with classroom rules and procedures.

BALANCED PARENTING

Background

These parents embrace many of the beneficial approaches mentioned in other styles by trying to balance their professional lives, family responsibilities, as well as other obligations. They realize the importance of schedules and organization because their lives are so busy. In many regards, this is what many parents aspire to be in our time. In today's society where there are so many obstacles and challenges in raising children, these parents desperately seek to find new and innovative ways to maximize time and make sure that they provide the appropriate guidance and direction in their children's lives.

They might also be described as:

- Sensitive
- Aware
- Responsible
- Considerate
- Great at multitasking

Examples

Balanced parents can come from professional or working-class families. Despite the busy schedules they are able to organize their families, they make every attempt to make sure that they attend to all of the needs of their children. They are great multi-taskers and can be found supporting their children at dance recitals, baseball games, and school plays.

Balanced parents work with whatever resources they have to make the most of their lives. For example, despite holding full-time jobs and raising three children, these parents still manage to keep Sunday evening for family meal time. Despite the scheduling challenges that this may present, they feel that coming together as a family for a weekly ritual is much more important.

Some additional examples of behaviors from this particular parenting style might also include the following:

- *Balanced parents* will attend all meetings that are required of them and may even be able to make additional ones.
- They will always show up on time for teacher conferences and parent meetings.
- These parents will find ways to change from their clothes at work to their coaching uniforms to be on time for practice.
- They tend to work cooperatively with educational professionals.

Possible Reasoning

These parents are aware of the importance that balance plays in a child's development as well as for their family. *Balanced parents* understand the value that personal and family obligations play, and wish to be positive role models for successful balance for their children. They view time as a very precious commodity and maximize quality time that they spend with their children. In addition to the quality time they spend with their families, they are also able to maintain relationships with friends and family. They realize that in order to fully experience life, an individual must be able to juggle his or her responsibilities so that the quality of life can be maximized.

Teachers might often hear the following things from these parents:

- "I will find the time to make it to the performance."

- "We set aside family time every week."
- "I work nights but I can rearrange my schedule so that I can attend."
- "My husband will be at the recital while I will go to the softball game."

How Educators Could Best Work with These Parents

Teachers should realize that these parents consider time to be very precious and expect it to be used properly. They welcome organization and frequent feedback that includes a variety of ways to provide communication. Due to their schedules, some of these parents may have to do a lot of their communication during after-work hours. In other situations, these parents will reorganize their schedules so that they can be available for their children for games, performances, and programs. *Balanced parents* are appreciative when teachers are understanding of their schedules and use their time efficiently.

A teacher might also:

- Keep good student records that include homework, phone and parent contacts, class participation tests grades, and performance, as well as how well their child is performing in relationship to the rest of the class or classes.
- In meeting with these parents, make sure to have a sufficient amount of examples and evidence to support what you want to share with them.
- Be prepared for the parent meeting, and make sure that you have all records and information that you think you will need.
- View the parent as a fellow team member and make sure to value his or her time.

THE FAITHFUL

Background

These parents use religion as the foundation of their parenting style as well as for how they govern their daily lives (Belkin, 2012). They rely on their respective faiths for guidance regarding many of the prescriptive rules of child rearing and ensure that those rules are being followed. Because this style encompasses all religions, these parents can be found throughout the United States. *Faithful parents* will impose the various rules promoted by their respective religions and use it as the foundation for many, if not all, of their decision making.

They might also be described as:

- Strict
- Faithful

- Caring
- Involved

Examples

In public schools, teachers will often come across parents who are firmly devout in their religious beliefs. In my experience, teachers have been very respectful of all faiths and make sure to accommodate their students' needs.

In most situations, *faithful parents* will communicate religious restrictions that may occur in the classroom. These parents carefully monitor their children's actions and in some cases even their diets. They are usually extremely devout and lead lives that exemplify the tenets of their faith. They may take their children out of school to celebrate their own holidays or observances. *Faithful parents* may also be concerned about activities in the classroom that are inconsistent with their beliefs.

For example, students from some religions are not permitted to celebrate birthday parties. Therefore, teachers must make the necessary provisions to make sure that arrangements are made for the day but more importantly that these things are communicated beforehand to all of the parents so that all children's beliefs are respected.

Some additional examples of behaviors from this particular parenting style might also include the following:

- Request the year's reading list well in advance to ensure that all titles do not conflict with their beliefs
- Want to be notified of any activity that may be inconsistent with their beliefs
- Try to have their teachers understand the basics of their religion to better understand how it impacts their students
- Are very proud of their religion and usually do not mind talking about it and sharing information with anyone who is curious
- Will stop by the school unannounced to make sure that their children, and sometimes the teacher, are respecting their religious beliefs

Possible Reasoning

Sometimes these parents are newly converted and in other cases their religion may go back generations in their families. In any event, these parents are compelled to honor the teachings of their faith and raise their children in a similar fashion. They are aware of the difficulties that this can sometimes present but feel that the rewards are worth it. They will modify their lives so that they can make their religion the focus of their family.

Teachers might often hear the following things from these parents:

- "Our religion does not allow that."
- "My people frown upon that type of behavior."
- "We don't allow our son to engage in those kinds of activities."
- "I'm sorry, but this book isn't appropriate for us."

How Educators Could Best Work with These Parents

This particular style can pose some challenges to teachers. Because of the wide variety of religions that exist in our country, it may be difficult to keep up with the modifications that could present themselves. Teachers are sometimes expected to know all of the specific rules and regulations for each religion that exists in their classrooms. This is obviously unrealistic. It is best when *faithful parents* establish good means of communication with their children's teachers.

The greatest challenge I have witnessed is when some children of *faithful parents* begin to veer from their religious ways. In some cases, teachers are put in the middle and expected to reprimand their children for straying while in school. Of course, teachers are not required to correct or reprimand a child who is doing things that other children are doing. In these situations, clear expectations for what a teacher will and will not be able to do must be communicated with their parents so that the parent-teacher relationship does not become adversarial.

A teacher may also:

- Find ways (newsletters, email, website, etc.) that provide information for parents and keeps them updated with what is going on in the classroom.
- Keep good student records that include homework, phone and parent contacts, class participation tests grades, and performance, as well as how well their child is performing in relationship to the rest of the class or classes
- Be proactive. Try to contact these parents before a problem arises or immediately when it does occur.
- Being open minded is an important part of being a teacher. In many cases, we will interact with a multitude of cultures. In doing so, there may be times where cultures clash and put us in very challenging situations. It is always good to role-play about how you would handle situations before they even occur to prepare for the changing times.

GOLDEN AGE PARENTING

Background

This type of parenting refers to a traditional model that consists of one parent staying at home while the other works. The benefits of this approach are that it provides stability and structure in a time where most families must have both parents working to make ends meet. Due to the variety of different types of families that currently exist in our country, this style could take on many different appearances. For example, there can be the old-fashioned father out working while a mother stays at home and is the homemaker. Conversely, there are many households where the father stays at home and the mother works full time. In addition, there may also be homosexual and transgender families where there are two mothers, two fathers, one transgender, or any combination thereof.

They might also be described as:

- Old-fashioned
- Traditional
- Strict
- Conservative
- Attentive

Examples

Golden age parents are a return to the previous generation where two-parent households were common in our country. These parents may look much different from their previous counterparts, but they still seek to assume one parent as the chief economic provider while the other assumes the majority of the parenting responsibilities. They can be found volunteering with school functions and extracurricular activities. They have very close bonds with their children and are cohesive families.

Some additional examples of behaviors from this particular parenting style might include the following:

- They will pick their children up and drop them off when they can.
- They don't mind being contacted by the school. In fact, these parents enjoy phone calls, both good and bad. Because they have made sacrifices to allow one parent to be home, they will be on top of situations before they get out of control.
- *Golden age parents* understand that raising children can pose challenges, and they are willing to accept those challenges.

- They will return phone calls immediately. These parents understand the importance of communication and will respond to teacher requests.

Possible Reasoning

These families seek to try to provide the stability that they feel will best help their children in economic times that usually require wages from both parents. For wealthier families, this poses fewer economic issues. In other cases, families with less financial resources find themselves making many sacrifices in order to provide this kind of lifestyle for their children: vacations may be less frequent, living arrangements much more humble, and the extras kept to a minimum.

Golden age parents feel that the old way of parenting was the most effective. They are fully aware of the problems that can come from having one parent assume the financial responsibilities but feel that the benefits of having an actual parent raise a child instead of someone outside the family is well worth it.

Teachers might often hear the following things from these parents:

- "We will be there."
- "We like to be involved."
- "One of us will be definitely there."
- "We like to do those things ourselves."

How Educators Could Best Work with These Parents

Educators are recommended to form partnerships with these parents because they are usually willing to volunteer their time. These parents tend to appreciate feedback and are usually very supportive of the teachers and the school system. They accept any criticism from the school and seek ways to help their children improve. They have high expectations for their children and do not rely solely on the school system to plan for their children's future.

The only time these parents will become negative is when a lack of communication from the teacher creates a problem that could have been easily addressed. In these times, most teachers just assume that both parents are at work during the day. These parents make it abundantly clear that they are available and will become upset if there is an opportunity for them to address an issue but couldn't because the teacher forgot that they were available. After all, from the parent's perspective that is one of the reasons they decided to stay home in the first place.

A teacher might also:

- Reflect on prior conversations and be careful what you say. These parents tend to remember every word and will reference it when needed.
- Try not to promise something that might not be possible to deliver.
- Keep good student records that include homework, phone and parent contacts, class participation tests grades, and performance, as well as how well their child is performing in relationship to the rest of the class or classes.
- Be proactive. Try to contact these parents before a problem arises or immediately when it does occur.

INSTINCTIVE PARENTING

Background

The basic tenet of *instinctive parenting* stems from the belief that all parents instinctually know the right thing to do in raising a child (McGolerick, 2011). Although some may view this as more common sense than anything else, it differs from *hyper-parenting* styles in that there isn't a mad rush to try to compensate for things. Comparatively, it also differs from *hypo-parenting* styles in that there is a very large degree of attentiveness. In most cases, however, it is usually most often heavily influenced by the parents' own upbringing.

These parents may be aware of all of the parenting techniques but instead rely on what they think is best for their children. This approach draws heavily from a traditional authoritative approach, as explained by Baumrind (1967), and is not easily swayed by current parenting fads. These parents also tend to have ways of doing things that have been passed down from one generation to the next.

They might also be described as:

- Pragmatic
- Sensible
- Moderate
- Reasonable

Examples

These parents are fairly open to the strategies and disciplines of other approaches but rely heavily on what they feel is best for them and their family. They tend to rely on judgment and experience as the foundation for how they raise their children and aren't as concerned with how they may be perceived. For example, toilet training can always be a sensitive issue with parenting. Each style may have its own approach to best practices concerning this activity. *Instinctive parents* rely not only on what worked in their past but also on whatever works best for their children in the present. They may borrow from other approaches if they feel that it is more beneficial to them.

Some additional examples of behaviors from this particular parenting style might also include:

- Will call the teacher to keep in contact with progress
- Will only intervene with the school when they do not understand a decision
- Will act on hunches or feelings about things with their children
- Will ask for advice about certain parenting situations

Possible Reasoning

The philosophy of the *instinctive parent* is a combination of two schools of thought: *if it isn't broken why fix it?* and *different strokes for different folks.* In many regards, this isn't a problem if the parents are open-minded and understand that today's children are confronted with a set of challenges that didn't exist for previous generations. For as good as these parents can be, they are only as good as their ability to accept certain changes that are happening in the world and their ability to adapt to the new rules that have emerged.

For example, when I was a teenager if someone started a rumor about someone else it rarely expanded outside of his circle of friends. Today, teenagers have the ability to broadcast a message to potentially millions of people. The traditional way of dealing with someone spreading rumors just doesn't work at today's level. It is only with the sound judgment and adaptability that an *instinctive parent* will be able to address the situation accordingly.

Teachers might often hear the following things from these parents:

- "I just don't think that's what is best for my child."
- "What do you think is the right way of doing it?"
- "I'll think about that."
- "Most of parenting is just good old-fashioned common sense."

How Educators Could Best Work with These Parents

In working with these parents, teachers should realize that they will not be dazzled by statistics and research. *Instinctive parents* usually have their own philosophy regarding what is best for their children. In some cases, they may not see the potential for their own children because they have focused on their own opinion of what they should be. These parents tend to not want to overanalyze things and may not acknowledge problems that may develop with their children by implementing proactive strategies. They may disagree with educators but usually it comes from their own experiences and not being blinded by some ulterior motive.

A teacher might also:

- Listen carefully to the parents to better understand their position regarding certain subjects.
- When a teacher witnesses a change in the student, assist parents with that adjustment.
- Choose opportune times to intervene with these parents. In certain cases, it may be best to be selective about what student behaviors a teacher wants to address.
- Create partnerships with these parents. They may not be easily convinced that their way is not the only way but can be persuaded with reason and persistence.

THE MISSIONAL PARENT

Background

Helen Lee describes in her writings that the *missional parent* is a faith-based parenting style in which mothers raise their children to be socially conscious. The author also goes on to state that this style reinforces the teachings of their respective faiths by demonstrating to their children the balance of school, church, and volunteering (2010). The major difference with this style and *faithful parenting* is that *missional parents* tend to be a little more liberal and emphasize the role of volunteering as it impacts community awareness and involvement. They use their respective religions as a basic foundation for their parenting styles but are not as conservative with how they administer discipline to their children.

They might also be described as:

- Spiritual
- Kind
- Devout
- Good-natured
- Involved

Examples

Missional parents can be very protective of their children and impose high moral standards on them. They are concerned about their children succeeding academically but place a high regard on their behaviors. They model kindness, generosity, and compassion, and expect their children to act the same way. *Missional parents* are also usually involved in community services where they can be found volunteering their time and are very loyal to their local church.

These parents will model how they expect their children to act by performing acts of community service as well as assuming leadership positions in civic organizations. They will expect, but not necessarily coerce, their children into volunteerism by bringing them to all of the events that they attend.

Some additional examples of behaviors from this particular parenting style might also include the following:

- Gently remind teachers of the tenants of their faith but will not be excessive in their interactions with school officials
- Will teach their children about tolerance and the importance of acknowledging all cultures and faiths
- Don't expect everyone to think the same way they do and teach their children the value of respect and good moral character

Possible Reasoning

These parents rely on faith as the foundation for how they conduct their lives, but they are also not oblivious to what is happening in the world. They do not struggle with religion for themselves but sometimes struggle with their children embracing it with the same fervor. Unlike *faithful parents*, these parents will not impose their religions on their children as they get older. They usually feel that they have provided them with the tools that they need and now the rest will be up to them. They have the desire to try and help the world be a better place, and believe that through their religion and community involvement they can accomplish this goal and be a productive member of society.

Teachers might often hear the following things from these parents:

- "What can we do to help?"
- "He used to listen to us all of the time."
- "I know she's good."
- "I will talk to my priest about this."

How Educators Could Best Work with These Parents

Teachers will usually work quite well with these parents. They are very articulate about their faith but also aware of all of the challenges that occur in society that confront children. They might periodically remind teachers about potential conflicts with the school curriculum and their religion, although this is not frequent. The most difficult times will occur when these children reach adolescence and decide not to follow the religion of their parents. Teachers are recommended to maintain good communication with these parents and keep them abreast of things that occur within the classroom.

Missional parents can sometimes have high expectations for teachers and school communities. They understand that religion is not the focus of education but feel that character is an integral part of schooling that is missing from the curriculum today. They may offer suggestions and opportunities for the school to get involved with the community.

A teacher might also:

- Be prepared for the parent meeting, and make sure that you have all records and information that you think you will need.
- Maintain accurate student records and have them handy.
- Communicate classroom events and activities via email, school website, or other social networking.
- Find ways to connect the classroom and the community to address ways of improving where they live.

PUNISHMENT-BASED PARENTING

Background

This style harkens back to a time of the strict authoritarian parent as referenced by Diana Baumrind (Gershoff, 2002). These are extremely strict parents who do not tolerate any aberrant behavior from their children. They establish rules and expect their children to follow those rules without question. They do not believe in feelings and emotions as much as they do about raising obedient children. They tend to be very firm in their approach and are oblivious to criticism from their peers or professionals.

Although this style might seem better suited for the *divergent parenting* category, it more closely resembles the way that some parents from yesteryear raised their children. Although it may seem hard to believe now, there was a time that many parents ruled with an iron fist. This was also a time when the words *emotions*, *self-esteem*, and *feelings*, were very seldom mentioned when discussing ways of parenting.

They might also be described as:

- Strict
- Unflappable
- Demanding

- Curt
- Heavy-handed

Examples

At one time in the distant past, it seemed that many parents might have fit the profile of *punishment-based parents*. These parents ruled their houses with an iron fist and would expect their children to be very obedient. They would discipline their children, even physically, in public without regard for other people's perceptions or opinions. There was little discussion regarding children's mistakes or how they could do things differently the next time. Children were expected to learn based on the discipline they received. If they did something and a punishment wasn't given, they knew they were doing what their parents thought was right. If they received punishment, it meant that what they did was wrong and they were disciplined accordingly.

Today, these parents will most often not be so flagrant about disciplining their children in public but still impose harsh penalties for their disobedience. They proceed with much the same philosophy of using discipline as the primary teaching tool in parenting their children.

Some additional examples of behaviors from this particular parenting style might include:

- Bragging at how tough they are on their children.
- Scolding their children in public regardless if they are around their peers or other parents.
- Expecting their children to not give in to their emotions. *Punishment-based parents* expect their children to be strong and take their punishment with honor.
- Not being overly sensitive to their children's feelings and emotions. These parents acknowledge that feelings exist but do not place a high regard on sentimentality when it comes to raising their children.

Possible Reasoning

These parents have a philosophy that the old-fashioned, heavy-handed discipline produced better results when raising children. They mostly feel that children today are far too spoiled and believe that only through rules and discipline will they be able to succeed. They are critical of many of the things in the world and may not have much control in their own professional lives; they may wish to establish control in their households.

In some instances, they adopt this parenting approach because it is more closely aligned to their own personality of maintaining control and order. In other instances, they may act this way because *punishment-based parenting* is much more black and white. This approach is much more concise and immediate than many other approaches.

Teachers might often hear the following things from these parents:

- "I know how to discipline my child so you don't have to tell me."
- "If the other parents discipline their children like I did, your job would be a lot easier."
- "Kids today need more discipline."
- "I forbid my children to do such things."

How Educators Could Best Work with These Parents

Punishment-based parents can be very strict, and it is usually because of this that problems can be seen in the classroom. If their punishments become too excessive, they can affect the children in many negative ways. Teachers, of course, are trained to identify these indicators and are instructed to report them to the proper authorities if suspicions of abuse arise. These indicators are often seen more in the younger grades but could also appear during adolescence as well.

I have encountered some *punishment-based parents* who try to be very intimidating to teachers and are not always cordial to them. They can be abrasive, curt, and sometimes rude when trying to get their way. Educators are recommended to always have sufficient information whenever they meet with them and encourage meetings to be held where others can monitor them.

A teacher might also:

- Try to use language that addresses the student's specific behavior and is not something that can be interpreted as critiquing the parent.
- Always speak in the positive when possible. You can say the same things in the positive instead of presenting them in the negative.
- Don't generalize. Do not say, "he doesn't do any homework" when you can say, "he has not completed fifteen of the possible twenty homework assignments."
- Do not be afraid to professionally disagree with the parent. Although the phrase "let's agree to disagree" has become quite cliché, it is a reality. The goal of every parent meeting should be to reach some sort of agreement, but there will always be the outliers where agreement just is not possible. Know when a conversation is going around in circles and move on to the next topic.

SLOW PARENTING

Background

This style was first proposed by journalist Carl Honoré and prescribes that children should be given time for free play and for family bonding (2005). This approach is in direct contrast to the fast-paced society of today and seeks to go back to a more traditional style of parenting. *Slow parenting* harkens back to a much simpler time where parenting was viewed much less of a chore and more of something that is treasured. These parents are not in a hurry to have their children grow up, nor are they in a rush in their own lives. These parents see the importance of taking their time in child rearing. Despite all of the stimuli today, they do everything in their power to slow things down and try to approach parenting with sensibility.

They might also be described as:

- Thoughtful
- Sensitive
- Focused
- Diligent
- Understanding

Examples

These parents still see the value in lazy afternoons, family drives, and Sunday afternoon picnics. They do not need all of the bells and whistles of other styles and tend to enjoy being in the company of their children. They try their best to slow down the fast-paced nature of today's society that poses many challenges to prolonged times for family activities.

Slow parents will engage in things that allow for time and reflection. They shut out certain aspects of society that they find harmful or unproductive and focus on more of the things that increase the quality time they spend with their families.

Some additional examples of behaviors from this particular parenting style might also include:

- Taking vacations to places that allow them to spend quality time together. These locales may not be the most expensive but provide opportunities for the families to bond and relax with each other.
- Spending more time discussing things that warrant it.
- Making sure they eat dinner together either every day or specific days of the week.
- Participating in such family activities as technology-free Sundays.

Possible Reasoning

These parents don't see anything wrong with the old days when families spent most of their time together entertaining themselves. They wish society could slow down a little bit so that they can appreciate the *now* and enjoy life.

They are aware of the distractions of today but also see the value in spending quality time with each other. They are not afraid of hard work and realize that parenting is not easy and may take time in addressing certain behaviors, but they also feel that only through strong familial bonds that are made from spending time with each other can really effective parenting be accomplished.

Teachers might often hear the following things from these parents:

- "I like talking to my daughter. I enjoy her company."
- "We celebrate our holidays together as a family."
- "We all come out to his baseball games."
- "This weekend we're going camping!"

How Educators Could Best Work with These Parents

These parents are usually easy to get along with for the most part. They like to be kept informed about how their children are doing in school because they want them to be successful and happy in life. They are easy to communicate with and also are collaborative. *Slow parents* value professionalism in their children's teachers. *Slow parents* understand that anything that is worthwhile takes time and cutting corners doesn't always guarantee success. They do not look for easy answers and expect some things to take time to accomplish

A teacher might also:

- Establish clear class learning objectives and make them accessible to parents.
- Be sensitive and listen carefully, critically, and reflectively to parent concerns and complaints. What might start out as sounding like a complaint may turn into a plea for help.
- Keep good student records that include homework, phone and parent contacts, class participation tests grades, and performance, as well as how well their child is performing in relationship to the rest of the class or classes.
- Be proactive. Try to contact these parents before a problem arises or immediately when it does occur.

Chapter Seven

Millennial Parenting

Millennial parenting can best be described as a variety of approaches that include a number of parenting styles that encompass the diversity of today's society. These styles represent the many different varieties of cultures and socioeconomic backgrounds that currently exist in America. Although these parents are not necessarily specific to the new millennium, they do represent what may be viewed as styles that are specific and unique to this era that is comprised of technology, the Internet, diversity, and an emphasis on global awareness.

The approaches that will be detailed in the following pages are comprised of some interesting titles that represent such themes as global awareness, multitasking, going green, overachieving, and living in the information age.

These parents are often perceived as:

- Technology driven
- Research based
- Bloggers
- Information hoarders
- Meta-aware
- Self-aware
- Reflective

AMERICAN DREAMERS

Background

American dream parents tend to be from working-class families who understand the value of hard work and preparation (Belkin, 2012). They have aspirations for their children to do much better than they achieved in life and will work very hard to ensure that that they help their children get the opportunities that were never afforded to them. They tend to dedicate most if not all of their resources to making sure that their children are provided with all of the opportunities they may have never had. These parents will invest all of their resources, time, and energy to making sure that their children are attended to. They are not comprised of any specific ethnic group and can be found in many cultures across the country.

They might also be described as:

• Overly optimistic
• Unrealistic
• Opportunistic
• Idealistic

Examples

American dreamers set high expectations for their children and expect the schools to help them fulfill their aspirations. They will involve their children in a variety of activities that they feel will help them succeed later in life. For example, the parents might join local community service groups because they believe that their membership will improve the odds of receiving scholarships the groups provide.

They may also involve their children in specific sports or activities that they feel will be able to propel them to success in later years. They understand that athletic prowess is one way of attaining social status as well as potential scholarships when they attend college.

Some additional examples of behaviors from this particular parenting style might also include:

• Parents who believe their child is a star athlete. In most cases, it will not matter that professionals might contradict them.
• Students who set unrealistic expectations with the urging of their parents.
• Parents who encourage their children to participate in things they do not like to do.

Possible Reasoning

In many cases, these parents are so unfulfilled with their own level of success that they become consumed with the planning of their children's futures. They differ from *tiger moms* because of this overwhelming desire to see their children succeed way past their own level of success and are more similar to *investment parents* in their desire to have their children prosper. Unlike *in-*

vestment parents, *American dreamers* do not necessarily plan a specific way for their children to succeed but just see success as a means to an end. Their motivation comes from a sincere desire to have their children lead a better life than they did. This only becomes an issue when these parents lose perspective and become excessive and extreme.

Teachers might often hear the following things from these parents:

- "We know he's going to be successful and come back to help us out."
- "She can do anything she wants to do."
- "He deserves to be more successful. It's the American way!"
- "It's never too late to start planning to attend an Ivy League school."

How Educators Could Best Work with These Parents

These parents are highly motivated and will sacrifice whatever they can to ensure that their children achieve. They tend to be supportive of schools but sometimes become frustrated when they don't feel like their children are receiving all of the advantages that other students receive. They can also become easily disgruntled and dissatisfied when their children aren't progressing to the levels they desire.

Teachers are encouraged to provide data when available to curious parents who wish to know where their children rank locally, regionally, and nationally. Approaching these conversations frankly and objectively will provide these parents with information that is important.

A teacher might also do the following:

- Do not engage the parent in discussion of how other teachers in the past or present work with your student. You can, however, ask how another teacher was successful in addressing specific behaviors or areas of need.
- Don't generalize. Do not say "he doesn't do any homework" when you can say "he has not completed fifteen of the possible twenty homework assignments."
- Do not be afraid to professionally disagree with the parent. Although the phrase "let's agree to disagree" has become quite cliché, it is a reality. The goal of every parent meeting should be to reach some sort of agreement, but there will always be the outliers where agreement just is not possible. Know when a conversation is going around in circles and move on to the next topic.

AWARE PARENTING

Background

This style is similar to *attachment parenting* in many ways but differs regarding some specific criteria (Solter, 1989). *Aware parents* recognize the importance of play, laughter, and crying in the context of a loving parent/child relationship. Research for this parenting style is based on the work of Aletha Solter, and this style of parent places an emphasis on the following criteria. These parents are attentive and respectful of their children's emotions, especially when it comes to their own individuality. *Attachment parents* look to keep a child at a certain level of dependence, whereas *aware parents* will embrace either dependent or independent children with the same enthusiasm.

They might also be described as:

- Emotionally attentive
- Responsive
- Supportive
- Communicative

Examples

Aware parents may participate in many of the same conventions as *green parents*, *hot tub parents*, and *mindful parents* when it comes to applying parenting skills to each of their children. They can often be seen rationalizing with their children at an early age, discussing things with them, and being aware of their child's emotional strengths and weaknesses. They are very perceptive that children can be different and address them with the variations they think will help the children be happy.

Some additional examples of behaviors from this particular parenting style might also include:

- Believing in natural childbirth
- Subscribing to nonpunitive discipline and peaceful conflict resolution through family meetings and mediation
- Recommending prompt responsiveness to crying
- Using a reward system with their children

Possible Reasoning

Much like their name implies, *aware parents* are cognizant of the many challenges that face families today and simply seek to provide the best parenting they can for their children. They realize that each child is unique and what may work for one may not necessarily work for another. They realize that their approach may have to change over time and when circumstances, such as additional siblings, impact the family structure. They are aware of their children's academic, social, and emotional growth, and treat each child with the time and support he or she deserves. These parents may not always succeed, but they are determined to play a significant role in their children's lives and will modify their approach to better serve their children and the goal of making them successful.

Teachers might often hear the following things from these parents:

- "I think I know what he wants."
- "I don't believe in strict discipline."
- "We need to have a family meeting about this."
- "What do you think she needs?"

How Educators Could Best Work with These Parents

These parents do not require as much attention as some of the other parents covered previously. However, they do like to be kept informed of their children. They realize that not all children will attain academic success but they encourage their children to try their best at whatever they do. *Aware parents* believe themselves to be in tune with their children's needs and may only conflict with teachers when there is discrepancy between the two adults. They will be very vocal advocates for their children and will encourage them to do the same.

A teacher might also:

- Be prepared for the parent meeting, and make sure that you have all records and information that you think you will need.
- Be sensitive and listen carefully, critically, and reflectively to parent concerns and complaints. What might start out as sounding like a complaint may turn into a plea for help.
- Develop and work on long-term goals for the students in conjunction with the parents.

BOOK OF THE MONTH (BESTSELLER) PARENTING

Background

Bestseller parents suffer from the inundation of information that is produced through print, media, and the Internet. Their motives are well-intended and can be very beneficial if the strategies that are implemented are given sufficient time to be successful. As the name suggests, these parents are extremely well-informed and seek out best practices as well as the hot new parenting approaches that seem to be produced on an ongoing basis.

They may subscribe to blogs, read new books, or be part of interest groups that profess one idea over another. In addition, they often change their style depending on what book they are reading and what other parents are doing (Sotonoff, 2011). They try their best to stay on top of current parenting trends and research to better raise their children, but they lack consistency.

They might also be described as:

- Impressionable
- Easily manipulated
- Fashionable
- Capricious
- Curious

Examples

Bestseller parents will quite often be very vocal about the current approach and espouse all of its newfound virtues. One month, they will extol a token reward system for their children; the next month, they will focus on assertive discipline. After reading about *permissive parenting*, they might try it out in their own family. If that doesn't work, they might next try *tiger parenting*. The rules for the children change on a frequent basis. In most of my experiences, these parents never seem to find the right fit for their families. In most cases, I found the children just become older and develop independently of their parents' attempts. I liken these parents to those who are constantly looking for the perfect diet. They move from one fad to the next in the hope of finding the one that is perfect for them. Much like the *bestseller parents*, this usually never happens.

Some additional examples of behaviors from this particular parenting style might also include:

- Parents who change their minds frequently
- Students who get confused
- Parents who become inconsistent and unclear with what they want
- Lack of organization
- No enactment of long-term plans

Possible Reasoning

Bestseller parents have the best intentions but lack the patience and discipline to focus on one particular approach. In their personal lives, they may exhibit similar characteristics of capriciousness as well. They lose interest quickly and are not known to commit to things. Perhaps they are looking for quick fixes or cutting corners. As most parents already know, there are very few shortcuts in raising children. They often do not see the value of executing plans but would rather spend most of their time planning instead of actually doing what they say they are going to do.

Teachers might often hear the following things from these parents:

- "I tried that already. It doesn't work."
- "Nothing seems to work with her."
- "Any new ways I can get my kid to listen to me?"
- "I just don't get how some people make it work."

How Educators Could Best Work with These Parents

These parents may pose some unique challenges to teachers because of their inconsistencies. They may make certain requests in the beginning of the school year and only a few months later may have contradicting instructions. Beginning teachers will be surprised when they first encounter these kinds of parents, but seasoned veterans usually know the best ways of addressing their needs. Teachers are recommended to document things the best they can, including meetings, conferences, etc. This will allow teachers to produce written documentation of parental requests so that they can keep these things clear to all parties.

A teacher might also:

- Establish clear class learning objectives that are made accessible to parents.
- Be sensitive and listen carefully, critically, and reflectively to parent concerns and complaints. What might start out as sounding like a complaint may turn into a plea for help.
- Try not to promise something that might not be possible to deliver.
- Create actions plans for students when necessary.

BUTTERFLY PARENT

Background

Annie Burnside's book *Soul to Soul Parenting: A Guide to Raising a Spiritually Conscious Family* is the basis for this specific style of parenting. This approach is characterized by nurturing the transformation of a child into a conscious global citizen who is emotionally and spiritually aware (2010). These parents place a high importance on the interconnectedness of the world and how their children play a part in the global consciousness.

Butterfly parents tend to be more concerned with how adjusted their children are than their academic progress. This is not to say that these parents do not care about academics; rather, they feel that there is a greater emphasis on having their children be good people who can interact with a variety of cultures and backgrounds.

They might also be described as:

- Nurturing
- Setting high expectations
- Globally conscious
- Compassionate
- Altruistic

Examples

These parents enjoy multicultural activities and can be seen encouraging their children to have play dates with children of different backgrounds. They will also be involved in Earth Day and as well as other global and sometimes political demonstrations. They thrive on diversity and cherish the time that they spend with their children.

Butterfly parents believe that helping shape globally aware citizens is an obligation, and they take it very seriously. They encourage good behavior and cultivate these characteristics in their children.

Some additional examples of behaviors from this particular parenting style might include the following:

- These parents will encourage their children to volunteer.
- They might be involved in organized religion, but not always.
- These parents will be interested in how their children act toward other children as well as adults.
- Children might take on caretaker roles for other siblings, relatives, or neighbors.

Possible Reasoning

These parents are very interested in global concerns and desperately want their children to make a difference in the world. They feel that their children are a means to address the world's troubles and that enlightening them will help feed their souls. They tend to be very sensitive people who are not prone to arguments or finger pointing. They have a sincere desire to be positive and encourage their children to do the same.

Teachers might often hear the following things from these parents:

- "We care how she interacts with other people."
- "We think that her volunteer work is what we are proudest of."
- "Our child has a very good heart."
- "We encourage him to volunteer."

How Educators Could Best Work with These Parents

These parents crave for their children to be involved in addressing global issues and would love to see more of it included in the school curriculum. Therefore, when teachers include real-world scenarios and encourage problem solving, these parents are sure to be very encouraged. Unlike some other types of parents, these parents do not mind hearing the truth but will still continue to try and have their children involved. They are devoted and enjoy the opportunity of working with teachers to help make their children better people and better global citizens.

A teacher might also:

- Know when to ask for an outside perspective such as a veteran teacher, a supervisor, or an administrator.
- Create actions plans for students when necessary.
- Take notes during parent meetings.
- Ask for parent suggestions for classroom activities when appropriate.

DRY CLEANER PARENTS

Background

Dry cleaner parents leave much of the child rearing to others such as teachers, nannies, or daycare workers. Tim Elmore explores these parents in his book *Generation iY: Our Last Chance to Save Their Future* (2010). These parents will spend a considerable amount of money on various activities for their children to engage in but prefer not to handle the major responsibilities of child rearing themselves. They handle most of their challenges in life with money and expect to do the same with their own children. If used with love and support, this style can be very beneficial, but when it is used due to lack of parental support, it can have some negative effects.

Dry cleaner parents are often very successful in their careers and usually are from higher socioeconomic groups. They are very competent in their professional lives and see the value in allowing "experts" who are better trained than they are assume certain aspects of training their children. In most situations, they view themselves as managers of their children.

They might also be described as:

- Intelligent
- Motivated
- Accomplished
- Facilitators

Examples

Dry cleaner parents can be found to seek a variety of services for their children from an early age. For example, they may enroll their children in full-day prekindergarten, karate, dance, piano lessons, and play groups on a regular basis. Although many parents today involve their children in a number of actives, *dry cleaner parents* rely mostly on the services of others to raise their children. They simply add the finishing touches and reinforce what others have done for them. They may be lenient or strict, and will most often lean on any of the other styles as the basis for the how they conduct themselves.

These parents will hire personal trainers to help improve their child's pitching style or batting swing. Other times they might send their children to the most expensive dance studios. They will use their resources to support their children by either developing or refining their talents or interests.

Some additional examples of behaviors from this particular parenting style might also include:

- Parents who enroll their children in after-school activities every day
- The sense that these parents may not enjoy alone time with their children
- Referring certain parenting responsibilities to the adults who they pay to work with their children
- Parents who think that every problem they have with their child can be solved with money

Possible Reasoning

In many cases, these parents may either be intimidated by the work it takes to raise a child or would just simply prefer not to tackle the challenges, and would prefer to have others assume many, if not all, of these responsibilities. I have witnessed several different types of parents also morph into this approach. For example, there are some parents who are interested in adopting the *tiger parent* approach but lack many of the skills necessary to do so and instead outsource all of this to others. When the parents carefully facilitate and supervise, there is a direction. When these parents have others care for their children, they may do so because they do not wish to be around their children for long periods of time.

There are also some extreme examples of *dry cleaner parents* who use these supplemental adults for other means. In these cases, they are actually trying to minimize the time they spend with their children because they view parenting as much too time consuming for them.

Teachers might often hear the following things from these parents:

- "We have never really had to deal with that before."
- "Can you recommend someone we can send her to?"
- "What are we going to do? What are *you* going to do?"
- "I don't think that's our job as parents! That is your job as the teacher to try and figure it out."

How Educators Could Best Work with These Parents

One of the major challenges teachers may face with *dry cleaner parents* is that they often mistake the services they procure for their children as a symbol of their devotion to them. If these parents don't take the time to form bonds with their children, they will do so with the other adults in their lives because nothing can really take the place of parental attention.

Teachers are encouraged to solicit these parents to attend parent-teacher association meetings and participate in classroom projects to get them more involved in the day-to-day activities of their children. They should also remind these parents that their participation is more important than them being experts in something. Asking for parent input is important and can establish an approach where shareholders are valued and respected.

A teacher might also:

- Try to use language that addresses the student's specific behavior and not something that can be interpreted as critiquing the parent.
- Suggest activities that these parents can do with their children at home. Use vacation time for children to interview their parents and get to know them and their pasts.
- Encourage students to find out about their parents' occupations and what they do for a living.
- Promote *Take Your Child to Work Day*.

ENGAGED PROGRESSIVES

Background

These are the types of parents who view tolerance as the fundamental core of their approach (Belkin, 2012). Instead of a cohesive philosophy, these parents do not subscribe to a specific belief but rather view personal freedom for themselves as well as their children as essential to living. Of course, they also believe in consequences from one's actions as well, and they see this role as providing children with the opportunity to begin decision making at an early age. These parents engage themselves in their children's lives and affairs and believe in personal freedoms. They are interested in raising children who can be good decision makers on their own and will become adults who are problem solvers. They might follow a mantra of do no harm as a general philosophy for their approach and will often do what they feel is right in regards to raising their children.

They might also be described as:

- Honest
- Open
- Empathic
- Grounded
- Fair

Examples

These parents are progressive in their thinking and usually expect their children to be responsible people. They are less likely to use punishments and tend to provide clear guidelines for their children to follow. They set clear boundaries and are not afraid to get their hands dirty.

Engaged progressives will expect their children to be more mature than other children because of the liberties provided to them throughout their lives. They are aware of all of the ills and trappings of society today like drug abuse, teen pregnancy, and such but still forge ahead to what they feel is the right way to raise their children. They try to tie some of the common sense from the traditional era of parenting to address many of the problems that are being faced by children today.

Some additional examples of behaviors from this particular parenting style might also include the following:

- Parents will extend curfews for their children, but these parents also expect their children to earn their trust.
- Children from these families will have chores and responsibilities at home.
- Children of *engaged progressives* will be encouraged to have jobs outside of the home and learn how to balance responsibilities.
- Punishments are commensurate with infraction and are not given without provocation or in anger.

Possible Reasoning

These parents also feel that many of the problems today can be solved, rather than caused, by today's technology. They confront the challenges of today head on and do not hide behind the glory days of the past. They are pragmatic and understand that times have changed but also realize that much can be done today to still hold onto ideals and personal responsibility. They are stern when they need to be and compassionate when they need to be.

They believe in the system and find America to be a great place to raise a child. They do not see technology as a curse but will find ways to use it to improve their lives. Although their children might have cell phones at an early age, these parents might require that they check in at required times.

Teachers might often hear the following things from these parents:

- "I expect better from her. She knows right from wrong."
- "When you finish your homework then you can watch television."
- "I think you're old enough to make the right decision."

How Educators Could Best Work with These Parents

Teachers should be reminded that these parents are strong advocates of allowing their children to make choices even at an early age. These children tend to be responsible and will most often tend to teachers' directions. Conferences with these parents should be organized and focus on behaviors and how to improve their children behaviorally or academically. Only in certain instances may these parents need to be reminded of age appropriateness in allowing their children to make these decisions.

Engaged progressives promote responsibility and maturity with their children. They tend to role model these behaviors for them and expect them to be reinforced while in school. They enjoy seeing that their children's classes are organized and provide opportunities for their children to assume jobs and tasks that help them become successful.

A teacher might also:

- Establish clear class learning objectives and make them accessible to parents.
- Be prepared for the parent meeting, and make sure that you have all records and information that you think you will need.
- Take notes during parent meetings. *Engaged progressives* will be very clear about their expectations of their children.

SERENITY METHOD

Background

B. Caplan published *Selfish Reasons to Have More Kids: Why Being a Great Parent is Less Work and More Fun Than You Think*, which explained this approach in greater detail (2012). This approach lends its name from the *serenity prayer*, which advises the speaker to change the things that he or she can change and accept the things that he or she cannot change.

    Serenity parents differ from *free range parents* in that they will try to change what they feel they can with their children and abandon other things. In some cases, this can be very liberating in situations where parents are forced to accept behaviors or limitations that affect their children. In other cases, this can pose several problems for the parents as well as their teachers.

    They might also be described as:

- Accepting
- Sensitive
- Nonconfrontational
- Free-spirited
- Nonjudgmental

Examples

These parents may allow certain behaviors because they feel that it is something beyond their control or may even be the limitation or handicaps of the child. For example, I have seen this approach adopted by parents of children with disabilities, eating disorders, and behavioral issues. It may appear that they are giving up on their children but, more accurately, they are giving up on the things that think they no longer can control. This *serenity* can happen at any age of the child but most often can be seen in the early adolescent years.

    Some additional examples of behaviors from this particular parenting style might include:

- Will not indulge in bad behavior but accept it as part of their children's personality
- Will draw some very interesting boundaries on behaviors they will address with their children
- Will only help their children with certain things when they ask their parents for assistance
- May secretly wish for their child to change but believe it is just the way he or she is

Possible Reasoning

These parents are concerned that overcorrecting their children may stifle their individuality. These parents do not necessarily hide from challenges in their own lives but will definitely only tackle the ones they think they can handle. They are compassionate and understanding but sometimes this can be to their children's detriment. They are not blind to problems their children have but have made peace with themselves that it is beyond their power to change them. Never is this more apparent than with children who have bad attitudes. Because these behaviors are not sufficiently addressed at early ages, they can spiral out of control as the child gets older. These parents have a high threshold for accepting things and when tantrums or other things like this occur in public, onlookers will often be amazed.

Teachers might often hear the following things from these parents:

- "He's always been that way."
- "We tried to stop her from doing that but that's just her way, I guess."
- "I know he can be very impatient and have tantrums, but he also has a very generous side to him as well."
- "No sense in trying to change her now, that's just her way."

How Educators Could Best Work with These Parents

Teachers may find that these parents sometimes will give up on some of the behaviors of their children that need the most attention. Often, these negative behaviors will manifest themselves in the classroom and provide some challenges to the classroom teachers. It is recommended that teachers establish clear rules and procedures for their classes and that these are shared with the parents. Frequent feedback regarding student progress and behavior is also critical to developing positive working relationships with these parents.

A teacher might also:

- Understand that empathy is okay, but sympathy is not.
- View the parent as a fellow team member.
- Always speak in the positive when possible. You can say the same things in the positive instead of presenting them in the negative.
- Maintain the mantra that this parent loves his or her child. Although some parents can be challenging, it is always important to retain focus and stay professional.

ENTITLEMENT PARENTS

Background

Entitlement parents pride themselves on being very informed and aware of educational services available to their children. They will take every opportunity to utilize these services even if their children do not necessarily need them. They tend to profess that because they are entitled to these services, they will take full advantage of them. They are informed of their rights and are extremely familiar with policies and procedures at the local, state, and federal levels. In extreme cases, they use their knowledge and assertiveness to intimidate teachers and school officials to get their way.

On one end of the spectrum, these parents can be applauded for their conscientiousness regarding their children's needs and ensuring that they are provided. In extreme cases, they can become opportunists who take resources just because they can, regardless of whether they are truly needed or not.

They might also be described as:

- Self-centered
- Self-righteous
- Industrious
- Confrontational
- Manipulative

Examples

Entitlement parents are extremely informed regarding the school's responsibilities and what they must provide for their children. They will fully utilize these services and complain if they are not provided. When these services are actually required by the child, most professionals understand. It is when these services are being utilized when they aren't necessary that it is an obvious attempt of the parent to attain them for self-serving reasons.

There are some parents who are able to navigate through the school system to manipulate for their own means. For example, I have unfortunately witnessed many parents of students with disabilities ask for things in the child's Individualized Education Plan that would actually give them advantages over the rest of the class. I have witnessed *entitlement parents* manipulate the system to receive additional tutoring, assistive devices, and a myriad of other services.

They are very outspoken and will find ways for themselves to assume quasi-leadership positions to advance their agenda. At public meetings, they will quite often refer to better services provided by other schools in neighboring towns. They will go to great lengths to ensure that they do everything in their power to get what they want.

Some additional examples of behaviors from this particular parenting style might include:

- Always looking for freebies
- Taking more than they contribute
- Will not volunteer for anything that doesn't advance their power or their reputation
- Will bully and intimidate other parents and teachers as well

Possible Reasoning

Entitlement parents have many of the characteristics of *hyper-parents* in that they remove as many challenges from their children's lives as they can, but they differ in that they tend to be more methodical and manipulative in the execution of their agendas. In my conversation with many of these parents, I have found that they firmly believe that the educational system is severely flawed and will not naturally do what is right for children unless they are being carefully watched. Although they may claim that they are out for the interests of all children, they are mostly concerned just about their children.

Teachers might often hear the following things from these parents:

- "I know the law."
- "I read the district policies, and you are not following them."
- "If I have to, I will go to the newspaper and let them know what is going on in the schools in our community."
- "Well, we're just going to have to see about that!"

How Educators Could Best Work with These Parents

Entitlement parents can pose some challenges for the classroom teacher. They will engage teachers in arguments and constantly test the boundaries of what they are able to get away with. These parents also have a tendency to move from one teacher to the next or one school to the next until they get what they are looking for. They are not afraid of ruining a teacher's career in the process. In their minds, they have reconciled with themselves that what they are doing is just and they will stop at nothing to get what they want. They tend to see everything as a battle, and they always fight to win. Teachers who are not adept at confrontations will easily crumble to these parents.

A teacher might also:

- Maintain the mantra that this parent loves his or her child.

- Try to move your button every day. We all know that there are people who make it their mission in life to perturb others. Do not be baited into trigger words that you know will cause you to lose your professional perspective.
- Take notes during parent meetings. *Entitlement parents* can use your words against you.
- Always be professional.
- Don't generalize. Do not say "he doesn't do any homework" when you can say "he has not completed fifteen of the possible twenty homework assignments."
- Have a policy for unannounced, impromptu meetings. For example, meetings can run no longer than twenty minutes.
- Know the child's pertinent information. If the child has an IEP or 504, make sure that you are familiar with what is written and make sure that you are in compliance.
- Know when to ask for an outside perspective such as a veteran teacher, a supervisor, or an administrator.

FAST FOOD PARENTING

Background

Due to the many pressures that exist in our society today, a great number of parents have been forced to be put into this category. Parenting has become very difficult, especially when one considers that the family has undergone many changes in America. The two-parent houses that do exist are often faced with the challenge of both parents working to make ends meet. This poses many problems because the availability of parents can be very difficult to achieve.

This title refers to the fast food culture that has been forced to speed everything up in order to fit everything into their lives. Families move at a rapid pace and even rush their quality time. These parents differ from the *balanced parents* in that although both categories attempt to accomplish the same goal of providing every resource and time with their children, the *fast food parent* isn't always as successful.

They might also be described as:

- Stressed
- Frenetic
- Caring
- Listless
- Tired

Examples

These are the parents who try to fit everything in and in some cases have to cut corners just to keep things moving along. For example, in some situations, parents have to drop their children off at prekindergarten and also enroll them in after care. That means that in these situations the parents are without their children for more than eight to ten hours a day.

Fast food parents can be found having rather hectic schedules where they go from work, to baseball practice picking up one child, then off to dance rehearsals where they pick up the other child. On the way home, they may pull into a restaurant to grab a bite to eat. Once home, the parents take turns checking the homework while balancing other chores like laundry, packing lunches, and paying bills. Every day is full of activities and juggling. In between these things, parents try to find quality time to actually connect with their children through discussion and sharing.

Some additional examples of behaviors from this particular parenting style might also include:

• Checking homework on the car ride to school
• Forgetting things
• Being late to work, school, or programs
• Rushing through things

Possible Reasoning

These parents want the best for their families but feel forced, due to professional obligations, to minimize the time that they spend with their families. They realize that quality time is important so they try their hardest to participate in their children's lives. In doing so, these parents often have to cut corners to accomplish their goals. For example, the well-balanced nutritional dinner that they would like to prepare for their children might have to be substituted with fast food instead. In other cases, the parents may spend the least amount of time reviewing their children's homework because of their own late hours. They have learned the art of multitasking but always fear that they are missing out on something important in their children's lives.

Teachers might often hear the following things from these parents:

• "I'm trying the best I can."
• "There just doesn't ever seem to be enough time."
• "We've been trying to get around to doing that."
• "My job just called me into work ..."

How Educators Could Best Work with These Parents

Teachers are advised that these parents are usually very efficient and appreciate spending their time wisely. Because they become so concerned with accomplishing things, they sometimes lose sight of the fact that raising children takes time. These parents sometimes are very frustrated because they never feel like they are able to provide for their family the time that they truly deserve. Perhaps the most important thing that teachers can do when interacting with *fast food parents* is to acknowledge that these parents are under pressure and are trying their best to address their children's needs.

A teacher might also:

- Establish clear class learning objectives and make them accessible to parents.
- Be sensitive and listen carefully, critically, and reflectively to parent concerns and complaints. What might start out as sounding like a complaint may turn into a plea for help.
- In meeting with these parents, make sure to have a sufficient amount of examples and evidence to support what you want to share with them.
- Be prepared for the parent meeting, and make sure that you have all records and information that you think you will need.
- Reflect on prior conversations and be careful what you say. These parents tend to remember every word and will reference it when needed.

GREEN PARENTING

Background

This style of parenting attracts individuals whose primary concern centers around the environment and reducing the carbon footprints that we leave. *Green parents* exhibit some of the characteristics of their 1960s *flower parent* antecedents, but they are armed with more information and many more causes (Gross, 2013). For example, they may endorse birthing at home, using cloth diapers, and practicing prolonged breastfeeding.

They are also similar to *butterfly parents* with the possible distinction that taking care of the planet is their contribution to the universal movement. These parents will also look for all-natural alternatives to aid in their parenting tasks and will usually place their children on very specific diets.

They might also be described as:

- Globally conscious
- Generally cooperative
- Loving

- Fanatic

Examples

These parents seek homeopathic alternatives, are ardent recyclers, and are always on the lookout for new causes to pursue. They make decisions about most things in their lives around the philosophy of environmentalism and conservation, and most often raise their children in the same fashion. They practice what they preach and will always find ways to try to convince others to adopt their ways.

Green parents can be found participating in a variety of community activities that involve improving the environment. For example, they may protest against deforestation, offshore drilling, the need for better recycling programs, or other pertinent issues. They most often bring their children to these events and start them at an early age to be involved in community affairs.

Some additional examples of behaviors from this particular parenting style might also include the following:

- Their children can have special all-natural diets.
- The parents may occasionally protest.
- The children may be very earthy.
- The parents will be very open-minded about most things.

Possible Reasoning

These parents may be first-, second-, or third-generation *green parents*, and they firmly believe in their way of life. They look to return to a more natural way of raising children and are not easily impressed with modern ways because of all of the negative things that are produced from progress. They enjoy working cohesively as a family, and their philosophy about life and the environment tends to bring them together. Because of this philosophy, they are often found to respect life and be more tolerant of others, even when it conflicts with their own beliefs.

Teachers might often hear the following things from these parents:

- "We're not really into that."
- "That's not necessarily our thing."
- "We would rather our children not engage in that kind of stuff."
- "The environment is very important to us."

How Educators Could Best Work with These Parents

Although *green parents* are concerned about the Earth, that doesn't mean that they neglect academics and extracurricular activities. These parents tend to have close relationships with their children and for the most part enjoy interacting with the school. They will work with their children's teachers and accept constrictive criticism when given. Teachers are recommended to continue engaging these parents in discussions about academics and other aspects of learning that work in conjunction to their civic-minded responsibilities.

A teacher might also:

- Be proactive. Try to contact these parents before a problem arises or immediately when it does occur.
- *Green parents* can be great supporters of initiatives that will improve the community. A class or school garden may be something they can assist in maintaining.
- Be sensitive and listen carefully, critically, and reflectively to parent concerns and complaints. What might start out as sounding like a complaint may turn into a plea for help.
- Reflect on prior conversations and be careful what you say. These parents are very passionate about their beliefs, even though some may be very different from the masses, and they take them very seriously.

MINDFUL PARENTING

Background

This style is similar to *attachment parenting* in that both styles focus on the importance on connecting emotionally with the child. They differ in that *mindful parenting* is about paying attention to the present, intentionally and without judgment. In their article on *mindful parenting*, Duncan, Coatsworth, and Greenberg describe that these parents take the time to engage their children (Naumberg, 2012). This engagement might include conversations, participation in their children's interests, volunteering in activities they want to pursue, or any type of engagement that improves communication between the parents and the children.

They might also be described as:

- Attentive listeners
- Nonjudgmental regarding themselves and their children
- Emotionally aware
- Compassionate

Examples

These parents are very in touch with their own emotions and try to do the same with their children. They live in the present and are known for their reflection and self-evaluation regarding their parenting. They may not always be perfect and have harmonious homes, but more often than not they strive to have balance and acknowledge the importance of communicating with each other. *Mindful parents* see the worthiness of spending time with their families and understand that problems are a part of life and confront them when they occur.

Some additional examples of behaviors from this particular parenting style might also include:

- Taking responsibility for their actions
- Acknowledging their mistakes
- Not being embarrassed to let their children know when they do something wrong
- Listening carefully to criticism

Possible Reasoning

These parents make a conscious effort to make sure that they are engaged with their children and take a very practical approach to raising children. They are aware that parenting can be challenging, but they face each challenge with optimism and poise. They have very little ego and will try their best not to let their emotions get involved in their parenting.

These parents consider their intellect and reason to be their greatest assets in parenting. They approach raising their children much like they do most other aspects of their life, with calm resolve and sound judgment.

Teachers might often hear the following things from these parents:

- "I think I made a mistake in letting her do that."
- "In looking back, I think we made a good decision in allowing him to go away with his friends."
- "Let's see if we made the right decision."

How Educators Could Best Work with These Parents

In my experience, I have found that many of the children of *mindful parents* tend to be more mature than their peers. These parents usually forge productive relationships with teachers and will be involved in their children's academic progress. They prefer frequent feedback and need to feel connected with the classroom teacher. As their children grow, the parents' roles will diminish as they encourage their children to take a more active role in their own education.

Mindful parents are open to criticism and work well with school officials. They are considerate, compassionate, and reflective. Teachers are recommended to keep these parents apprised of classroom activities as well as student progress. These parents will appreciate conversations rather than informal communication like emails or form letters.

A teacher might also:

- Take notes during parent meetings.
- Have a specific set of things you are willing to offer the parents (i.e., extra help, additional assignments, make-up work, daily or weekly contacts, etc.).
- Always be professional.
- Allot certain days during the year when parents can come in and see what their children are doing in school.

HOT TUB PARENTING

Background

This style can be perceived as an extension of the *best friend parent*, but it includes more of an advisory component than the former. First mentioned in a *The New York Times* blog, this parent professes to tackle some of the more difficult topics by talking through them with the child in a more relaxed and objective way (*The New York Times*, 2011a).

These parents take a different approach to parenting and see opportunities to talk things through with their children to address serious issues. These are not necessarily strict parents but they definitely care about their children and want them to succeed. These parents do not like to yell and on the surface are not extremely strict but offer more conciliatory parenting advice to their children. Unlike *best friend parents*, they have boundaries and rules in the homes but prefer to convince their children to do the right thing through conversations.

They might also be described as:

- Gregarious
- Down to Earth
- Conversational
- Sensitive
- Empathetic

Examples

Hot tub parents display many of the same characteristics as sitcom parents on television. They are usually calm, wise, and always have the right answers to life's questions. They do not enforce a long list of rules in their homes and feel that the best way to address problems with their children is through reason. On the surface, these parents may seem to operate in much the same way as *mindful, balanced,* and *available parents,* but their approach really defines itself in how they address problems and challenges they face in raising their children. Whereas other parenting styles may be stricter or more lenient, *hot tub parents* prefer to exercise their authority through means of reasoning and discussion.

Some additional examples of behaviors from this particular parenting style might also include:

- Waiting for the right time to talk to their kids
- Being mindful of not embarrassing their children in public or in front of their peers
- Doing things in their own time frame that seeks to maintain harmony within the family
- Being genuinely gentle people who care about their family as well as others

Possible Reasoning

These parents are not overly strict rule makers but prefer the opportunity for long talks, using persuasive conversational techniques to convince their children to do the right thing. These parents are usually very intelligent and feel that rationalizing with their children is the most effective way of disciplining them. In some cases, they are using the same tactics that their parents used in bringing them up. In other cases, it might be an opposite reaction to how they were raised. They have a philosophy that reason is enough to be able to persuade their children to act accordingly and do the right thing.

Teachers might often hear the following things from these parents:

- "I will talk to her about this when I get home."
- "I know he listens to me."
- "We have a very good relationship; I think we can reason with her."

How Educators Could Best Work with These Parents

Hot tub parents appreciate discussions with teachers about their children and often expect most adults to approach things the way they do. They may be surprised when discipline in any other manner is given. Some children from these homes may not be able to accept curt criticism because they become more used to detailed explanations about things. In some cases, these students may require more attention from their teachers. In other situations, they may mature earlier than their peers. Teachers are encouraged to use nonjudgmental language in interacting with these parents and to be prepared to provide details to better help them understand situations that occur.

A teacher might also:

- Clearly delineate parental responsibilities from school responsibilities.
- Try to use language that addresses the student's specific behavior and not something that can be interpreted as critiquing the parent.
- View the parent as a fellow team member.
- Always speak in the positive when possible. You can say the same things in the positive instead of presenting them in the negative.

PANDA PARENTING

Background

This style was created in response to the previously mentioned *tiger mom*. In one *New York Times* blog, a father referred to himself as a Panda Dad who was able to be cute and cuddly with his children but wasn't afraid to show some claw when necessary (2011b). These parents like to take of all of the high standards that have been professed by the *tiger parents* but also include some warmth and encouragement as well. They try to bridge the gap between being very demanding and aloof to understanding and encouraging. *Panda parents* can come across as very strong but also can be compassionate when necessary. They encourage their children to excel but try not to be so overwhelming that they cause their children discomfort or anxiety. They stress the importance of success, but do see it is as an ultimate goal and realize the importance of individuality. Their ultimate goal is to assist their children in reaching their full potential, whatever it may be.

They might also be described as:

- Firm
- Fair
- Consistent
- Even-tempered

Examples

Panda parents are similar to *backbone parents* as well as other *traditional/ neo-traditional* styles. They can be found to have strict rules and expectations for their children that may exceed many of the other parenting styles previously discussed. They are not easily satisfied with their children achieving the bare minimum of anything and will keep pushing them to challenge themselves. They will not be as excessive as *tiger parents* but definitely share the same enthusiasm for pushing their children to challenging themselves. They do not settle for less than their children's best and will set the bar very high for their children. They can be considered *tiger mom lite*, which is a more Americanized version that takes the children's emotional state into more consideration.

Some additional examples of behaviors from this particular parenting style might also include:

- Not being afraid to make difficult decisions for their children
- Being quick and swift when disciplining their children
- Overcorrecting their children
- Stressing the need for self-controlling behaviors in their children

Possible Reasoning

These parents constantly seek to find the balance between encouragement, being tough, being supportive, and also providing a loving and caring household where their children can flourish. They sometimes struggle with trying to find the right balance of being strict and being loving. In the best cases, they can handle it relatively well; in other cases, they can swing too far in each direction and spend a majority of their time trying to correct themselves. They see the need for direct supervision and direction to help their children in achieving success and preparing for their futures.

Teachers might often hear the following things from these parents:

- "We will handle it ourselves."
- "We're not too strict about that. The school is far too lenient"
- "Now's not the time to be too hard on her. We will wait a little while."
- "We are available to attend the event."

How Educators Could Best Work with These Parents

Teachers are encouraged to understand that these parents can sometimes vacillate between tough and forgiving. These parents don't mean to be mercurial but because of their approach they tend to go from very disciplined to very caring. When this type of behavior is not evident, these parents interact in much the same way as *tiger parents*. They have high expectations from the school system but will supplement their children's education with outside agencies if they feel it necessary to do so. *Panda parents* will sometimes challenge teachers and scrutinize the school curriculum to ensure that it is on par with other schools in the surrounding areas.

A teacher might also:

- Be sensitive and listen carefully, critically, and reflectively to parent concerns and complaints. What might start out as sounding like a complaint may turn into a plea for help.
- Keep good student records that include homework, phone and parent contacts, class participation tests grades, and performance, as well as how well their child is performing in relationship to the rest of the class or classes.
- Be proactive. Try to contact these parents before a problem arises or immediately when it does occur.
- In meeting with these parents, make sure to have a sufficient amount of examples and evidence to support what you want to share with them.

REDSHIRTING

Background

This approach is more of a tactic than an outright philosophy (Iannelli, n.d.). It is included here because it displays some of the characteristics of other parenting styles that have been covered but differs in that it is a strategy used to provide children with advantages over their peers. *Redshirting* is based on the premise that delaying a child will help him or her progress ahead of other students in his or her class. This style is based on the practice used in college sports where a delay or suspension of an athlete's participation is performed so that he or she might lengthen his or her period of eligibility.

Redshirting is most used by parents when they decide to hold back their child from starting kindergarten almost a year so that the child will be more likely to be further advanced than his or her peers. This has a reverberating effect that continues throughout the child's education.

They might also be described as:

- Manipulative
- Over-protective
- Calculating
- Ambitious

Examples

These parents will intentionally have their children start school later than they have to just to give their child a better advantage over other children. In some cases, these parents may use this tactic in other areas but I have not found this occurs that often. For example, if a parent moves his children from one karate school to another, he or she may decide to place his or her child in a lower ability level class so that his child can really experience success. Fortunately, there aren't too many situations where a child can be placed in these scenarios and as he or she gets older, it becomes less and less of an issue.

Some additional examples of behaviors from this particular parenting style might also include:

- Overinflating their children's egos
- Putting their children in situations they have already mastered
- Finding ways for their children to take re-tests of the same material
- Having their children preview courses and class materials so that they are more familiar than the rest of their peers

Possible Reasoning

In some cases, parents engage in *redshirting* because they may feel that their child needs an advantage because of a real or perceived deficit. Their action is based purely out of a need to provide their child with the ability to stay on track with his or her peers and not exacerbate this deficit. Some parents engage in *redshirting* for the desire for their children to have advantages to outperform their peers. They postulate that providing their child with early experiences of being advanced will set the tone for the rest of their professional lives. In short, they are trying to create an overachiever from the onset of his or her education.

Teachers might often hear the following things from these parents:

- "I think she needs another year in kindergarten."
- "He's not ready to move on."
- "Can she repeat it?"
- "I think you should give him the test again."

How Educators Could Best Work with These Parents

Redshirting may be a new term for middle and secondary teachers, but it is nothing new to early childhood educators. These grades are confronted with unique parenting challenges that include any tactic that can provide their child with more advantages. Of course, this scenario occurs naturally because of cut-off dates for kindergarten registration. Teachers will find *redshirting parents* posing certain challenges because they will sometimes seek for additional ways to assist their children in attaining any leverage in the classroom.

This is why frequent communication with parents is important to identify and address these behaviors. Teachers can advise *redshirting parents* of all of the supplemental programs and activities that can help their children advance in more productive ways.

A teacher might also:

- Establish clear class learning objectives and make them accessible to parents.
- Be prepared for the parent meeting, and make sure that you have all records and information that you think you will need.
- Know when to ask for an outside perspective such as a veteran teacher, a supervisor, or an administrator.
- Create actions plans for students when necessary.
- Provide additional activities and opportunities to assist the parents in helping their children succeed.

SUBMARINE PARENTING

Background

Deborah Skolnik coined this term for parents who remain hidden until their guidance is needed (2012). These parents stay close to their children and only intervene when they feel it is necessary to do so. Unlike like *Blackhawk* and *helicopter parents*, these parents try to have their children address many of their own challenges by themselves but are always on the lookout for possible danger. *Submarine parents* are not easily identified until there is a problem or situation. They tend to be generally cooperative parents who have very productive relationships with their children.

They might also be described as:

- Untrusting
- Deceptive
- Explosive
- Aggressive

Examples

Submarine parents may appear mild-mannered but will go into action within a moment's notice. They are much more professional and refined than *volcano parents* and aren't as mean-spirited as *snow plow parents*. For example, these parents may surface when their child is disciplined for something he or she did in the classroom. The teacher may be very surprised at the parent's reaction, having had only positive exchanges for the entire school year. *Sub-*

marine parents appear to be especially sensitive to certain triggers that can include discipline referrals, grades, or issues with other students. Recent legislation with harassment, intimidation, and bullying seems to have increased the number of irate reactions from parents who have otherwise been very supportive of public school systems.

Some additional examples of behaviors from this particular parenting style might also include:

- Not confronting teachers but going immediately to teachers' supervisors to resolve issues
- Being unpredictable in their actions
- Being vindictive in their revenge and indiscriminate with how they mete out their punishment

Possible Reasoning

As previously indicated, it appears that many of these parents are triggered by specific areas that cause them to react aggressively toward the school. I am certain that this may be because of the way these situations have been unsatisfactorily dealt with in the past or perhaps it may even indicate their own specific sensitivity to the particular issue. For example, I have encountered very reasonable parents who have become very antagonistic when their child has been accused of cheating. They provide excuses, argue, and even accuse the teacher of making up the entire incident. Most often, it is usually because they are being confronted with an aspect of their child they refuse to accept. As educators, we are all able to separate the behavior from the child, but for parents it is much harder to do so because it is their own child.

Teachers might often hear the following things from these parents:

- "You don't want me to have to follow-up on you!"
- "Don't underestimate us."
- "I knew you would pull something like this."
- "My son's record has never shown anything like this before."

How Educators Could Best Work with These Parents

Submarine parents only surface when challenges present themselves. In many cases, these parents may never surface during their child's education. But when they do surface, teachers will at first be quite surprised. The best preparation for teachers is to first acknowledge the probability of these parents appearing on a somewhat regular basis. Due to the spontaneous nature of these parents, teachers should also be prepared for these outbursts to occur anytime during the year, even the last few days of school. Once these parents have surfaced, teachers can identify them immediately and try to be as calm as possible to listen for their exact concerns. Like *volcano parents*, *submarine parents'* actual concerns may to be difficult to identify.

A teacher might also:

- Do not be afraid to professionally disagree with the parent. Although the phrase "let's agree to disagree" has become quite cliché, it is a reality. The goal of every parent meeting should be to reach some sort of agreement, but there will always be the outliers where agreement just is not possible. Know when a conversation is going around in circles and move on to the next topic.
- Try not to give too much information that isn't pertinent to the current topic of the conference.
- Take notes during parent meetings. The information may be needed later on during the school year.

YES PARENTS

Background

Yes parents value every experience with their children and are determined to make every moment memorable (Sears, 2010). A *yes parent* tries to say *yes* to all of his or her child's requests unless there is a good reason to say no. This style attempts to teach the child the difference of right and wrong through the child's own instincts, and is in stark contrast to children who are told no as a typical response to their requests. The strategy behind these parents is that they believe that by saying yes they remove part of the fascination with children wanting things. They also instill in their children the ability to create their own boundaries. On the surface, they may appear to be very similar to *free range parents* but upon closer examination these actually want their children to learn through what they are doing and are very much concerned with the repercussions of their children's decisions.

They might also be described as:

- Secure
- Confident
- Trusting
- Risk takers

Examples

Yes parents may be the type of parents who allow their children to stay up all night without a curfew only to wake them up early the next morning to attend to household chores. They teach their children that they have to be responsible for the choices they make—good or bad. They will often provide their children opportunities to make decisions from an early age as a means to prepare them for challenges they will have later on in life. *Yes parents* will be very permissive but might also enforce penalties for bad decisions that they may make.

Some additional examples of behaviors from this particular parenting style might also include:

- Allowing their children to experience failure
- Not making excuses if their child misses a deadline
- Not taking compliments for their children's behaviors

Possible Reasoning

These parents have their own philosophy regarding how to raise their children. They realize the importance of having children imposing their own parameters because they feel that children learn better that way. They are firm believers in learning by doing and will permit their children to embark on their own decision making. In most cases, supervised risk taking can be very productive for young children, but unsupervised behavior can lead to disastrous results. *Yes parents* are firm believers in personal freedoms and pride that above most other things.

Teachers might often hear the following things from these parents:

- "Are you sure you're making a good decision?"
- "If you think that's best."
- "What do you think is the right thing to do?"

How Educators Could Best Work with These Parents

Yes parents tend to only clash with teachers when they feel that their children's rights to make decisions have been suppressed. They will most likely work cooperatively with teachers and not intervene regarding discipline issues. They will be receptive to feedback and respond productively to constructive criticism. In later years, these students could pose some problems due to the personal freedoms they have been afforded in their childhoods. Teachers' authority may be questioned and conflicts may occur if they are not addressed immediately. It is suggested that teachers establish clear rules and procedures regarding classroom behaviors and what types of discipline warrants parental contact.

A teacher might also:

- Have frequent meetings.
- Try to use language that addresses the student's specific behavior and not something that can be interpreted as critiquing the parent.
- Try to have the parent put in writing exactly what the problem or concern is, and make sure that subsequent conversations remain focused on addressing and resolving those specific issues before moving on to other concerns.
- Find ways (newsletters, email, website, etc.) that provide information for parents, and keep them updated with what is going on in the classroom.

Chapter Eight

Divergent Parenting

This last category contains the most disturbing and dysfunctional of the previously studied parenting styles. The term *divergent* refers to the negative behaviors exhibited by these parents that most people would consider irresponsible. The following styles will contain characteristics that, although sometimes disturbing, are unfortunately present in our society today.

In my experience, some of these parents adopt these styles willingly, while others are forced into them due to financial, emotional, or personal reasons. I believe that this is an important distinction because the parents who knowingly decided to adopt one of these following styles is reprehensible, while the parent who is forced into it can be pitied.

Unfortunately, *divergent parenting* is a reality for many children in our society today. They are confronted with physical and emotional abuse, addiction, poverty, and a host of other challenges that impact their development. Although the obstacles that they face are overwhelming, there are a surprising number of students who are somehow able to overcome these challenges and succeed despite them.

These parents are often perceived as:

- Irresponsible
- Immature
- Unreliable
- Pressured
- Angry
- Disgruntled

THE BULLIED PARENT

Background

Bullied parents live in fear of their own children. As surprising as this might sound, this fear can present itself emotionally or physically. For some of these parents, they may fear losing their child's love and respect. This manipulation on the part of the child can begin at a very early age and continue well into adulthood. For other parents, this can be a very real and harrowing fear of physical violence that most often occurs when the child enters adolescence. They fail to lead their children and provide positive role models for them. In turn, these children grow up without boundaries and little, if any, direction.

They might also be described as:

- Insecure
- Passive
- Guilty
- Victims

Examples

Bullied parents will have to little to no control over their children. Consequently, these children will place themselves in many situations that will have disastrous results, leaving the parents to look on in either shock or despair. *Bullied parents* will helplessly watch their children become involved in altercations with other students, drug addiction, and other negative behaviors. These children push around their parents and are used to assuming positions of control of their lives. These parents are usually oblivious to criticism from their own peers as well as from professionals from the school.

Some additional examples of behaviors from this particular parenting style might also include the following:

- Children of *bullied parents* could potentially pick on other children in the class.
- These parents will not address behaviors and ask teachers to do it instead.
- The students will be confrontational to any authority figure.

Possible Reasoning

It is difficult to comprehend how a parent can be put in these situations but unfortunately they do exist. In my years in education, I have encountered several *bullied parents*. The explanations vary, but most of these parents are riddled with fear that their children will either hurt them or, more often, hurt themselves. Most of the cases I have experienced involved children who had severe emotional problems that involved physical violence toward the parents. These parents differ from *parents in fear* because their children are much more manipulative and calculating. These parents may seek help but will need a great deal of assistance in order to regain control of their children.

Teachers might often hear the following things from these parents:

- "We just can't control her anymore."
- "He's always been very headstrong."
- "We don't like to get her angry."
- "It's just easier to do what she says."

How Educators Could Best Work with These Parents

These parents often seek out teachers for help and guidance in addressing their children's behaviors. Although these children can be very physical to their parents, they may not necessarily misbehave in the classroom. Some of these students are well aware that there are rules and will act accordingly. Others may present challenges to teachers because their negative behaviors have gone unchecked for so long.

If they have identified *bullied parents*, teachers should seek out counselors or administrators to assist them. These parents need much more support and guidance than could be expected of a classroom teacher.

A teacher might also:

- Do not engage the parent in discussion of how other teachers in the past or present work with your student. You can, however, ask how another teacher was successful in addressing specific behaviors or areas of need.
- Try to use language that addresses the student's specific behavior and not something that can be interpreted as critiquing the parent.
- Clearly delineate parental responsibilities from school responsibilities.
- Try to work with colleagues and administrators to have and update a list of recommended referral services to provide to parents.

THE DETACHED PARENT

Background

Detached parents remove themselves from the parenting experience emotionally, psychologically, and even physically (Belkin, 2012). They provide minimal supervision and limited support of their children. These parents seldom interfere with the children's affairs and will very rarely interact with the school unless necessary. This detachment may occur because of their own emotional or psychological impediments that prevent them from forging more productive relationships with their children.

They might also be described as:

- Distant
- Emotionally detached
- Troubled
- Unconcerned

Examples

Detached parents will spend very little time around their children. In some cases, the detached behavior exhibited by them may be a newer occurrence; in other cases, it may have always been there. In the latter case, these parents would have spent minimal time raising their children. Their children may be used to long periods of isolation and to raising their other siblings. These children will often find friends with very functional families and sometimes become attached to them. The children learn to fend for themselves at an early age and mature faster than their other peers.

Some additional examples of behaviors from this particular parenting style might also include the following:

- Parents may suffer from depression or other medical issues.
- Parents will provide the basic necessities for their children.
- Parents will be unreliable.
- Parents are not concerned about academics or success.

Possible Reasoning

Many of the parents that I would considered to be *detached* seemed to suffer from other psychological issues such as depression, post-traumatic stress disorder, and other similar ailments. These issues may be recent developments or more long-term issues. In my interactions with these parents, I never felt that there was conscious malevolence toward their children. It always appeared to me that they, for whatever reason, were just unable to fully engage in being a parent for their children.

Teachers might often hear the following things from these parents:

- "I really can't do that."
- "I don't get involved with their affairs at this age."
- "Sorry, but I can't."
- "I guess I'm just not that good at that."

How Educators Could Best Work with These Parents

These parents will complain very little to teachers and minimally involve themselves in their children's education. In most cases, they will often go overlooked because their children will not be vocal about their home life. They older they get, the more they get used to this way of living. These children may assume extreme behavior either being very quiet and demure or constantly seeking attention from adults and their peers. In either case, they develop coping skills very early in life and may go unnoticed by most teachers. Exposing these children to their peers and helping them forge friendships can help them develop their social skills. Keeping in contact with parents and keeping them informed and requiring feedback from them will keep them aware of their responsibilities.

A teacher might also:

- Have frequent parent meetings
- Try to work with colleagues and administrators to have and update a list of recommended referral services to provide to parents
- Clearly delineate parental responsibilities from school responsibilities
- Always be professional

DISAPPROVING PARENTS

Background

These parents deemphasize the importance of emotions (Gottman and Declaire, 1998). They tend to be more negative and are known to be harsh critics of their children. They constantly impose restrictions and demand conformity for things that sometimes do not make sense to most other parents. They feel that negative emotions are bad character traits that can be controlled. Overall, they believe that all emotions are weak and should be controlled. They stress these things in their parenting and expect their children to follow in much the same way. They do not tolerate their children showing negative emotions and will find a variety of ways to diminish or prevent this behavior.

They might also be described as:

- Angry
- Confrontational
- Demanding
- Hard to please

Examples

Disapproving parents will be seen harshly criticizing their children in public. They expect them to maintain composure at all times and are role models for this type of behavior. They are very structured people who are very much in control of their own emotions. They do not overreact and can be characterized by their cool and distant disposition. They believe that control is a virtue and wish to instill this in their own children. They view emotion, especially negative emotion, as an unproductive waste of time. Above all things, they desire their children to be obedient and in control of their emotional state at all times.

   Some additional examples of behaviors from this particular parenting style might also include:

- Not allowing children to attend parties
- Disapproving of their children involving themselves in anything they do not see having value and importance
- Not believing in frivolity
- Not providing encouragement to their children
- Being difficult at parent meetings

Possible Reasoning

These parents are usually emotionless themselves and do not see any benefit in being emotional with their children. They may suffer from their own psychological and emotional problems that prevent them from performing many of the parenting duties that they should. *Disapproving parents* are very negative people whose negativity usually permeates their entire lives. They have relatively few adult relationships, which solidifies their isolation. Lastly, they may also be in a toxic marriage that may have reverberating effects on the children in the family.

   Teachers might often hear the following things from these parents:

- "We don't like them doing that."
- "We don't approve of that at home."
- "That doesn't work for us."
- "He knows better than to act like that."
- "We expect her to maintain composure at all times."

How Educators Could Best Work with These Parents

Educators are recommended to keep in mind that these parents are neither remorseful nor ashamed regarding how they raise their children. They seldom solicit advice from teachers and will not be very receptive to criticism about their children or how they raise them. They can come across as uncooperative and distant. Consequently, they will often not be very involved in their children's academic lives. They are often so immersed in their own negativity that they view the entire world through the same lens.

Teachers are encouraged to maintain a professional and collegial tone with these parents in all situations. They should be addressed as stakeholders and expected to address some of the academic goals of the child.

A teacher might also:

- Establish clear class learning objectives and make them accessible to parents.
- Be sensitive and listen carefully, critically, and reflectively to parent concerns and complaints. What might start out as sounding like a complaint may turn into a plea for help.
- Be proactive. Try to contact these parents before a problem arises or immediately when it does occur.
- In meeting with these parents, make sure to have a sufficient amount of examples and evidence to support what you want to share with them.

DISABLING PARENTS

Background

This parent will exacerbate or even invent a child's impediment or disability in order to help the child either gain an advantage or appeal for emotional sympathy. They seem to feed off of the attention and do not view their actions as preventing their children from progressing. These parents can sometimes go to great lengths to ensure that everyone else perceives their child for the disabilities that he or she has. In some cases, the disabilities may be real; in other cases, the disability may be exacerbated. Lastly, sometimes parents may even invent the disabilities all together.

They might also be described as:

- Attention seekers
- Confrontational
- Intelligent
- Conniving

Examples

Disabling parents advocate for their child to receive special services when he or she actually does not need them. They will manipulate anyone they feel will be able to help them accomplish their goal. They will try to persuade as many as they can with their agenda and will often repeat themselves so often that others will begin to believe them as well. They frequent board meetings and any public event. They thrive on public meetings to help move their agenda forward.

Some additional examples of behaviors from this particular parenting style might also include:

- Secretly hurting their children so that they can get some attention
- Forcing the schools to test for disabilities and moving from district to district until they get the answer they desire
- Manipulating the teachers to see their perspective
- Understanding how the school system works and making it work to fulfill their agenda

Possible Reasoning

Many of these parents suffer from diagnosed or undiagnosed mental issues that cause them to view their children as having a disability that may not actually even exist. In the event that it does, these parents will exacerbate the issue so that they receive the attention they want. In fact, in most cases attention seems to be the underlying reason why these parents pursue this type of behavior, because it usually paints them in a very positive way.

Teachers might often hear the following things from these parents:

- "You may not see it, but I know she has a problem!"
- "He may not act this way at school but at home it's an entirely different story."
- "How much more proof do you need that she has a problem?"
- "Obviously you're just not qualified enough to see it."

How Educators Could Best Work with These Parents

Fortunately, in my experience I have encountered very few of these parents. Unfortunately, the few I did encounter spent a considerable amount of time and energy that never did anything to ever benefit the child. These parents tend to get so wrapped up in the worlds that they create, they genuinely believe that they are crusading for the rights of the children when in reality they are severally hampering the children's development. This situation is all the more real when the children begin to buy into their fictional disabilities and actually manifest the perceptions into real shortcomings.

Teachers are recommended to approach these parents with positivity and assist them as much as they feel that they can. *Disabling parents* will be very aware of their rights, similar to *entitlement parents*, and will look for any opportunity to expose the teacher or the school for doing something wrong if anyone gets in the way of their children receiving the services that the parents believe the children deserve.

A teacher may also:

- Keep good student records that include homework, phone and parent contacts, class participation tests grades, and performance as well as how well their child is performing in relationship to the rest of the class or classes.
- Reflect on prior conversations and be careful what you say. These parents tend to remember every word and will reference it when needed.
- Try not to promise something that might not be possible to deliver.
- Don't feel like you have to answer every question on the spot. Sometimes reflection or additional information is needed to give an appropriate response.
- Know when to ask for an outside perspective such as a veteran teacher, a supervisor, or an administrator.

DROPOUT PARENTS

Background

Dropout parents can be very deceptive (Elmore, 2011). Teachers will easily identity them as parents who start the school year off volunteering for activities only to disappear and drop out of sight weeks or months later. Obviously, this can occur for a variety of reasons but if there is a reoccurrence and repeated pattern of these behaviors, the parents can be classified as *dropouts*. These parents will exhibit this pattern in almost all aspects of their lives: sports teams, karate classes, church organizations, etc.

They might also be described as:

- Noncommittal
- Unreliable
- Resistant to change
- Uncommunicative

Examples

In my experience, these parents tend to always drop out when they are needed the most. Although they present themselves as sound and reliable, in a matter of time they turn out to be quite the opposite. In some cases, I have witnessed *dropout parents* start off highly motivated and involved only to disappear without notice. They can assume a variety of other parenting styles before they disappear and may even have reoccurring excuses that they use each time. These parents tend to move from one social circle to the next so that their patterns are not initially obvious.

Some additional examples of behaviors from this particular parenting style might also include:

- Parents who don't return phone calls
- Children with poor attendance rates
- Children who incorporate lack of commitment
- Children who value relationships with their peers more than with adults

Possible Reasoning

It is difficult to determine whether these parents have good intentions because once they drop out they rarely reappear. *Dropout parents* may lack follow-through in other parts of their lives as well. For example, these may be the parents that make lofty promises that never seem to materialize. In my experience, they seem to be oblivious to how they impact their children's lives or the lives of others around them.

Teachers might often hear the following things from these parents:

- "We don't have the time."
- "We have other responsibilities like paying bills."
- "Unlike other professions, I have to work a full day."
- "Isn't the school supposed to take care of that?"

How Educators Could Best Work with These Parents

Dropout parents can be very frustrating to teachers because of how their inconsistencies affect their students. When they are involved, they can be extremely helpful and cooperative but all of that easily disappears after time. Once identified, teachers should still reach out to these parents to help them return to the previous ways. In some situations, these parents have the best intentions but lack commitment in the follow-through. Letting them know that dropping out and coming back in is okay. Anything they can do to be a part of their children's education is extremely important and valued.

A teacher might also:

- Create actions plans for students when necessary.
- Try not to give too much information that isn't pertinent to the current topic of the conference.
- Try to figure out what your own emotional triggers may be and work on getting them under control. Sometimes conferences can get emotional and

spirited. Always stay in control and when necessary recommend reconvening at another time to continue discussions.
• Have a specific set of things you are willing to offer the parents (i.e., extra
help, additional assignments, make-up work, daily or weekly contacts,
etc.).

ENABLING PARENTS

Background

Enabling parents support their children's bad decisions and enable their
negative behaviors. In many cases, they will even make excuses for their
children's actions or even blame others for their children's faults. They never
appear aware of any negative aspects of their children and will never criticize
them. They sometimes can act like *groupie parents* or even *parents in fear*,
but they differ because *enabling parents* are seemingly accomplices to their
children's bad behavior.

These parents can also be very protective and will react harshly to anyone
who they perceive as an enemy. They like when their children are on top and
will help them in any way to maintain that position.

They might also be described as:

• Selfish
• Egotistical
• Focused
• Argumentative

Examples

These parents will make excuses for all of their children's bad behaviors.
When their children start a fight, they claim the other student was responsible. If their child is caught cheating, they will blame the teacher. If their
children are late for a project, they will make excuses. No matter what
occurs, these parents seldom take responsibility for their own actions. They
don't expect their children to assume responsibility for their actions either.
These parents can become very belligerent when confronted about their parenting and will often go on the offensive to attack someone.

Some additional examples of behaviors from this particular parenting
style might also include:

• Overlook their child when he or she starts a fight
• Will make excuses when their child does not turn in an assignment on
time

- Will not only defend but attack other adults and children if necessary to get their way
- Not only ignore their children's bad behavior, but in some cases encourage it or rationalize it

Possible Reasoning

It is hard to understand why a parent would condone bad behavior from their children. In some cases, I'm sure it has something to do with being afraid of saying no to their children and wanting to indulge every one of their requests. In any event, it seems that *enabling parents* seek to please their children and are blind to any of their faults. This may be due to their own need to want to please their children or the fear that they will not be loved by their children if they do not support them in every action.

Teachers might often hear the following things from these parents:

- "It was the other kid's fault. She started it!"
- "Well, as the teacher you should have been more definitive about the due date of the project."
- "Unlike you, I don't see a problem here."
- "They're just kids."

How Educators Could Best Work with These Parents

Unfortunately, teachers will constantly be at odds with these parents. *Enabling parents* are indiscriminate when it comes to where they project their blame and anger. Teachers are usually the easiest targets because they might be the only people who will venture to provide any constructive criticism of these children. *Enabling parents* will sometimes seek to prove these teachers wrong and sometimes even try to destroy their reputations and careers. In interacting with these parents, it is always best to keep accurate notes and documentation of all meetings. Teachers shouldn't be afraid to ask a veteran colleague or an administrator in working with these parents because they can be so vindictive.

A teacher might also:

- Always be professional.
- Do not engage the parent in discussion of how other teachers in the past or present work with your student. You can, however, ask how another teacher was successful in addressing specific behaviors or areas of need.
- Try to use language that addresses the student's specific behavior and not something that can be interpreted as critiquing the parent.

- Try to have the parent put in writing exactly what their problem or concern is and make sure that subsequent conversations remain focused on addressing and resolving it before moving on to to other concerns.

HIPPO PARENTING

Background

In a *New York Times* article, Lisa Belkin described this type of parent as one who would do anything to their child, even squashing their pride, just to prove a point (2011). This parenting differs from *free range* and other *hypo-parenting* styles in that even when these parents know that something could have very serious consequences, they still allow their child to continue just to prove a point. These parents have a tendency to be rough and aggressive in ways that do not allow for criticism from others. In some situations, these parents are trying to prove a point so that their children can learn something; in other cases, their actions may be more self-serving to satisfy their own egos.

They might also be described as:

- Harsh
- Critical
- Arrogant
- Strong-willed

Examples

Hippo parents can be very loud and demonstrative, feeling that their way of doing things is the only way of doing things. They can be found stifling their children from speaking, over-criticizing their children when they do something wrong, or exacerbating their disappointment with their children. Unlike other parents, *hippo parents* seem to take some level of satisfaction in seeing their children being humiliated and defeated. These actions could occur in public, like a softball game or performance, and can be reinforced in the privacy of their own homes.

Some additional examples of behaviors from this particular parenting style might also include:

- Berating their children for a simple mistake
- Not advocating for their children
- Never looking to reduce or ameliorate any punishment from the school
- Always pointing out to everyone how wrong their children are

Possible Reasoning

One could suggest that maybe these parents act aggressively because they push their children too hard and are overly critical. But unlike *tiger parents*, *hippos* seem to be more concerned with power and control than actually motivating their children to succeed. It is also possible these parents are also repeating patterns of behavior previously established in their own childhoods. They have very strong vindictive personalities that often pit them against their own children. It sometimes appears that only when their children fail do they feel some kind of satisfaction.

Teachers might often hear the following things from these parents:

- "He has to learn the hard way."
- "She makes her own choices, and we will not get herself out of whatever she does wrong."
- "If he's old enough to do it, he's old enough to pay the consequences."
- "Good for her. Now she has to figure out how to get herself out of it."

How Educators Could Best Work with These Parents

The actions of *hippo parents* always cause considerable alarm for classroom teachers. Their behaviors teeter on emotional and physical abuse that directly affects the student. In some situations, these children may already have shut down emotionally by the time they reach the teacher's class; in these cases, identification is harder to determine. This is why administrators always encourage teachers to interact with the students to monitor their emotional status. In addition, teachers can be cognizant of signs of abuse and neglect and act on them swiftly and accordingly.

A teacher might also:

- Try to use language that addresses the student's specific behavior and not something that can be interpreted as critiquing the parent.
- Clearly delineate parental responsibilities from school responsibilities.
- Always be professional.
- Be firm, fair, and consistent.

PARENTS IN FEAR

Background

This is perhaps one of most alarming parenting approaches because, in this style, parents are afraid of their own children. This fear can be real or imagined, with the parents fearful that the child will physically or emotionally retaliate against them. They may be so enamored by their own children that they live in constant fear that their children will not love them; in other extreme cases, they may have an actual fear of physicality.

They might also be described as:

- Loving
- Fearful
- Nervous
- Insecure

Examples

Parents in fear will act nervous and apprehensive around their children whether at home or in public. They will wince, cower, and sometimes flinch when their children are around them. They can be very helpful and attentive to their children but also will drop whatever they are doing in order to address their needs. They will often be manipulated emotionally and even financially by their children, and can be placed in very difficult situations. Even though they appear to be afraid of their own children, they can be very aggressive toward others who hold them accountable or question their parenting techniques.

Some additional examples of behaviors from this particular parenting style might also include:

- Parents who ask teachers not to tell them that they talked
- Children who make the rules
- Parents who provide weak excuses for their children's actions
- Children who are difficult to control in class

Possible Reasoning

As with many of the other approaches in this category, it is often difficult to ascertain exactly how these parents came to be this way. I have witnessed parents assume this approach because they feel that there is a threat that their children impose. These threats can manifest themselves either physically or emotionally. It is also possible that this parenting approach could also be cyclical and reminiscent of their own childhoods. For example, these parents may have been raised in fear themselves, or circumstances could have created a situation where the fear is losing the love of their child.

Teachers might often hear the following things from these parents:

- "Please don't tell her I said anything to you about this."

- "I would just rather not disappoint him by making him do something he doesn't want to do."
- "I guess I have never been very strict with her."
- "Could you tell him for me?"

How Educators Could Best Work with These Parents

Parents in fear are usually also fearful of any authority figure and will most often not be disrespectful to teachers. However, they cannot be reliable and may not always be helpful with school officials regarding situations with their children. They will lie and manipulate situations if they believe that it will benefit their children. It is the fear that their children will retaliate in some way that drives them to comply with their children's demands. Teachers will identify these parents easily but tend to be more impatient with them, feeling that they need to assume a more authoritative role.

A teacher might also:

- Try not to promise something that might not be possible to deliver.
- Don't feel like you have to answer every question on the spot. Sometimes reflection or additional information is needed to give an appropriate response.
- Be proactive. Try to contact these parents before a problem arises or immediately when it does occur.
- Try not to get in the middle of disputes between parent and parent or parent and child.

REVERSAL PARENTING

Background

Reversal parenting is based on the premise where the roles of a parent and her child have seemingly switched. For all intents and purposes, the child assumes maturity and responsibility while the parent is irresponsible and immature. This is a very peculiar dynamic in which the child takes the primary role in his or her education as well as additional responsibilities. This type of parenting could be the product of a situation in which the parent, due to medical, financial, or psychological reasons, cannot provide the parenting that is expected.

They might also be described as:

- Immature
- Insecure
- In denial of his or her situation

• Arrested development

Examples

It is difficult to determine who the parent is in these types of relationships. Most often, the children act much more mature than their own parents. In some cases, *reversal parents* are so caught up in their own arrested development that they can hardly take care of providing guidance and support for their own children (Sedacca, 2013). These parents tend to be more interested in how they appear to others than whether their children receive the support and guidance that they need. They may sometimes at first appear like *groupie parents* and *best friend parents*, but upon closer examination, it is obvious that these parents put their own desires first while their children are placed in positions where they must assume roles that require much more maturity than their peers.

Some additional examples of behaviors from this particular parenting style might also include:

• Children who take care of their siblings
• Parents who are absent
• Children who assume more responsibility for their actions than their peers
• Parents who are nonresponsive

Possible Reasoning

There may be many reasons why *reversal parents* refuse to accept responsibility. Most of the situations that I have encountered were due to parents having children at young ages. In these examples, the parents could be less than twenty years older than their own children. In these cases, these parents were very resentful and lacked the maturity and life skills that would help them be better role models to their children.

Teachers might often hear the following things from these parents:

• "He has always been very responsible for her age."
• "He just doesn't know how to have fun."
• "She is a little boring."
• "He takes things too seriously."

How Educators Could Best Work with These Parents

These parents can pose some unique challenges to teachers because they offer little in the way of assistance in helping their children. In most cases, their children are very mature and assume much more responsibility than would be imagined, and they often require little assistance for the teacher.

The real problem occurs when something happens and the parents are faced with real dilemmas that require prudent judgment. In my experience unfortunately, none of these parents have ever been able to rise to the occasion and assist their children when needed.

A teacher might also:

- Maintain the mantra that this parent loves his or her child.
- View the parent as a fellow team member.
- Clearly delineate parental responsibilities from school responsibilities.
- Try to use language that addresses the student's specific behavior and not something that can be interpreted as critiquing the parent.

DUPLICITOUS PARENTING

Background

This particular type of parenting is based on the way a child's public persona is the complete opposite of his or her personality at home. In this case, children seemingly have two personalities: the one at home and the one outside of the home. For example, in many cases children tend to be well-behaved with their parents but act in an entirely different way when away from them. There are some cases, however, where the reverse is true as well.

These parents might also be described as:

- Delusional
- Unaware
- Limited
- Uniformed

Examples

In most cases, these children are supposed angels at home and only act up when they are in school. In other cases, although rarer, the opposite could be true: they are very bad at home but for the most part either abide by school rules or do so comparatively speaking. I have had the opportunity to work with both types in my career.

Duplicitous parents have a preconceived idea of how their children behave at school because it is based on how they see them at home. They will often give teachers warning of expected behaviors and always talk about them in extreme descriptions.

Some additional examples of behaviors from this particular parenting style might also include:

- Parents expect to hear the worst from their children's teachers and are surprised when they hear good things about their children.
- Children will label themselves as bad in school.
- Children may have low self-esteem.
- Parents are shocked to hear that their children are bad at school.

Possible Reasoning

These parents do not have a sense of their children's true identities. What these children reveal to their parents at home is vastly different from what they display to the general public. These parents are often confused as to why the child doesn't act the same way in school and often do not initially believe the reports of their actions to be true.

These parents are often hard to convince how their children actually act in school because of their predetermined beliefs. Teachers can provide countless examples, but it often take several years before these parents will begin to understand that their children have different personalities in different settings. I have had countless experiences where I have warned parents of their children being involved in suspected criminal activity. I would base these suspicions not on personal biases but upon numerous student conversations and eyewitness. In many of these examples, if the parents had only listened to school officials, the futures of these students would be much better than what actually occurred.

Teachers might often hear the following things from these parents:

- "Not my child."
- "She never does that at home."
- "Are you sure we're talking about the same child?"
- "Maybe we have better control at home."

How Educators Could Best Work with These Parents

Duplicitous parents often have very tenuous relationships with their children's teachers. When they receive the initial reports of their children that run counter to their perceptions, initially these parents develop mistrust for their children's teachers. Teachers are encouraged to keep conversations with these parents very professional, focusing only on specific behaviors or issues. They are usually never convinced easily but may be persuaded when teachers can present information in an objective manner. In certain cases, consultations with previous teachers can be helpful in creating action plans to help the student succeed.

A teacher might also:

- Do not engage the parent in discussion of how other teachers in the past or present work with your student. You can, however, ask how another teacher was successful in addressing specific behaviors or areas of need.
- Try to use language that addresses the student's specific behavior and not something that can be interpreted as critiquing the parent.
- Always speak in the positive when possible. You can say the same things in the positive instead of presenting them in the negative.
- Don't generalize. Do not say "he doesn't do any homework" when you can say "he has not completed fifteen of the possible twenty homework assignments.

Final Thoughts

Parenting will always be a difficult task and no one is really sure whether they did a good job until their child emerges safely through adulthood and has their own children.

Almost all child rearing strategies, with some notable exceptions, seem to be well-intended and work within their unique family dynamics, but unlike previous generations, children are being produced from a more diverse variety of parenting styles. Although the styles described here have been given distinct labels, some of these approaches may be situational and change as the family dynamic changes. For example, a single-parent family could easily become a blended family, changing the entire structure and the way two parents address raising their children.

What will the future hold for the children of the *millennium* and what will become of the school systems? I'm not sure anyone could accurately predict how all of these different approaches will remain or change years from now. At this time, though, schools still seem to be the only place where children still have to follow the same sets of rules, regardless of how they are being raised.

One thing is for certain: it is important that educators understand the diversity that is occurring in homes across the country today because it will have a direct influence on our interactions in the classroom as well as our culture as a whole. In his essay "Self-Reliance," Ralph Waldo Emerson writes, "If I know your sect. I anticipate your argument." If we don't begin to understand the many sects that already exist in our society, we are going to have a lot more arguments in the future.

I'm often asked, "So what approach do you recommend?"

Most people do not like my response because it isn't as definitive as most people would like. I assume that many want to have a simple straightforward response that would give them some clear direction and advice to help them with their child rearing. Besides, an "expert's" advice could give them clear directions, which *bestseller parents*, especially, would like.

The approach that is most effective is whatever one forges strong bonds between parents and their children, and helps prepare children for a successful and happy life. The answer, as to most anything really important, is much more personal and individual a response. Putting the *divergent parenting* styles aside, the purpose of this book was to begin conversations regarding the diversity of parenting styles and how this variety can affect classroom teachers. Additionally, I believe that chronicling these styles is important because it reflects the culture of the time. It would be interesting to reflect upon these styles in a decade or so to see how many still exist. I predict, though, that there will be many more styles that we may not even be able to fathom based on our current experience. I hope that if you have reached this far you have begun to understand the complexity of parenting and how it relates to the business of education.

Appendix

A List of Strategies Referenced in this Book

- Establish clear class learning objectives and make them accessible to parents.
- Be sensitive and listen carefully, critically, and reflectively to parent concerns and complaints. What might start out as sounding like a complaint may turn into a plea for help.
- Keep good student records that include homework, phone and parent contacts, class participation tests grades, and performance as well as how well their child is performing in relationship to the rest of the class or classes.
- Be proactive. Try to contact these parents before a problem arises or immediately when it does occur.
- In meeting with these parents, make sure to have a sufficient amount of examples and evidence to support what you want to share with them.
- Be prepared for the parent meeting, and make sure that you have all records and information that you think you will need.
- Reflect on prior conversations and be careful what you say. These parents tend to remember every word and will reference it when needed.
- Try not to promise something that might not be possible to deliver.
- Don't feel like you have to answer every question on the spot. Sometimes reflection or additional information is needed to give an appropriate response.
- Don't be afraid to ask administrators to attend a meeting if you feel it is necessary.
- Remind parents that there is some information that you would rather not know.

- Don't get in the middle of disputes between parent and parent or parent and child.
- Set clear boundaries for parents regarding meetings, class visitations, and preferred methods of contact.
- Know when to ask for an outside perspective such as a veteran teacher, a supervisor, or an administrator.
- Create action plans for students when necessary.
- Be firm, fair, and consistent.
- Do not be afraid to professionally disagree with the parent. Although the phrase "let's agree to disagree" has become quite cliché, it is a reality. The goal of every parent meeting should be to reach some sort of agreement, but there will always be the outliers where agreement just is not possible. Know when a conversation is going around in circles and move on to the next topic.
- Try not to give too much information that isn't pertinent to the current topic of the conference.
- Maintain the mantra that this parent loves his or her child.
- Try to figure out what your emotional triggers may be and work on getting them under control. Sometimes conferences can get emotional and spirited. Always stay in control and when necessary recommend reconvening at another time to continue discussions.
- Take notes during parent meetings.
- Have a specific set of things you are willing to offer the parents (i.e., extra help, additional assignments, make-up work, daily or weekly contacts, etc.).
- Always be professional.
- Empathy is okay; sympathy is not.
- View the parent as a fellow team member.
- Always speak in the positive when possible. You can say the same things in the positive instead of presenting them in the negative.
- Don't generalize. Do not say "he doesn't do any homework" when you can say "he has not completed fifteen of the possible twenty homework assignments."
- Have a policy for unannounced, impromptu meetings. For example, meetings can run no longer than twenty minutes.
- Know the child's pertinent information. If the child has an IEP (Individualized Learning Plan) or accommodations with a 504 Plan, make sure that you are familiar with what is written in it and that you are in compliance.
- Do not engage the parent in discussion of how other teachers in the past or present work with your student. You can, however, ask how another teacher was successful in addressing specific behaviors or areas of need.
- Try to use language that addresses the student's specific behavior and not something that can be interpreted as critiquing the parent.

- Try to have the parent put in writing exactly what the problem or concern is and make sure that subsequent conversations remain focused on addressing and resolving it before moving on to other concerns.
- Find ways (newsletters, email, website, etc.) that provide information for parents and keep them updated with what is going on in the classroom.

References

Adler, A. (1937). How position in the family constellation influences life-style. *International Journal of Individual Psychology* 3, 211-227.

Aldrich, C., and M. Aldrich. (1938). *Babies are Human Beings.* New York: The Macmillan Co.

Baumrind, D. (1967). Child care practices anteceding three patterns of preschool behavior. *Genetic Psychology Monographs, 75(1).*

Bean, S. (2010). What's your parenting style? Retrieved from http://www.parenting.com/blogs/show-and-tell/shawn-bean/whats-your-parenting-style?src=soc&lnk=rss.

Belkin, L. (2011). Calling mom a hippo. *The New York Times, November 28.*

Belkin, L. (2012). Parenting styles defined in new report on "family culture." Retrieved from http://www.huffingtonpost.com/2012/11/15/which-kind-of-parent-are-you_n_2137667.html.

Borgman, L. (2011). There are all types of moms. *Buffalo News* [Buffalo, N.Y] 31 Jan: C.5.

Burnside, A. (2010). *Soul to Soul Parenting: A Guide to Raising a Spiritually Conscious Family.* Deadwood: Wyatt-MacKenzie.

Caplan, B. (2012). *Selfish Reasons to Have More Kids: Why Being a Great Parent is Less Work and More Fun Than You Think.* New York: Basic Books.

Chua, A. (2011). *Battle Hymn of the Tiger Mother.* New York: Penguin Press.

Cline, F., and J. Fay. (1990). *Parenting with Love and Logic: Teaching Children Responsibility.* Colorado Springs: Pinon Press.

Coll, S. (2007). Helicopter parenting: Spiraling out of control. *The Washington Post,* 04 March: B.1.

Duffy, J. (2011). *The Available Parent: Radical Optimism for Raising Teens and Tweens.* Poulsbo: Viva.

Elmore, D. T. (2011). How to fix parenting styles which may damage your kids. Retrieved from http://www.howtolearn.com/2011/05/how-to-fix-parenting-styles-which-may-damage-your-kids/.

Elmore, T. (2010). *Generation iY: Our Last Chance to Save Their Future.* Atlanta, GA: Poet Gardener Publishing.

Emerson, R. W. "Self- Reliance." *Norton Anthology of American Literature. Shorter Fourth Edition.* New York: W. W. Norton, 1995, 492-508.

Gershoff, E. (2002). Corporal punishment by parents and associated child behaviors and experiences: A meta-analytic and theoretical review. Retrieved from http://www.repeal43.org/docs/Gershoff meta-analytic review:02.pdf.

Ginther, D., and R. Pollak. (2004) Family structure and children's educational outcomes: Blended families, stylized facts, and descriptive regressions. *Demography, 41(4),* pp. 671–696.

Goldsmith, B. (2013). Hyper-parents can make college aged children depressed-study. Retrieved from http://www.reuters.com/article/2013/02/13/us-parents-students-idUS-BRE91C18520130213.

Gottman, J., and J. Declaire. (1998). *Raising an Emotionally Intelligent Child: The Heart of Parenting*. New York: Simon and Schuster.

Gross, J. (2013). Introducing the latest lunatic parenting trend: Diaper-free baby rearing. Retrieved from http://www.slate.com/blogs/xx_factor/2013/04/22/elimination_communication_or_ec_parenting_lets_babies_go_diaperless.html.

Hellmich, N. (2004). Parents want to be teens' pals; But loose style can backfire. *USA Today*, 12 Oct: D.8.

Hodgkinson, T. (2010). *The Idle Parent: Why Laid-Back Parents Raise Happier and Healthier Kids*. Tarcher Publishing.

Honoré, C. (2005). *In Praise of Slowness*. Retrieved from http://www.carlhonore.com/books/in-praise-of-slowness/.

Hougaard, B. (2004). Curlingföräldrar och servicebarn, Debat om vort nye bornesyn ("Curling [a winter sport played on ice]. Parents and service children: Debate about our new view on children"). Stockholm: Prisma.

Iannelli, V. (n.d.). Parenting styles and parenting fads. Retrieved from http://pediatrics.about.com/od/parentingadvice/a/109_ptg_styles.htm

Lareau, A. (2011). *Unequal Childhoods: Class, Race, and Family Life*. Berkeley and Los Angeles, CA: University of California Press.

Lynd, R., and H. Lynd. (1929). *Middletown: A Study in Contemporary American Culture*. New York: Harcourt, Brace & Co.

Lee, H. (2010). *The Missional Mom: Living with Purpose at Home & in the World*. Chicago: Moody Publishers.

Leon, L. (2013). What's your parenting style? Retrieved from http://www.modernmom.com/blogs/lissette-leon-psyd/what-s-your-parenting-style.

Lynd, 1929.

McGolerick, E. W. (2011). 5 parenting styles for a new generation. Retrieved from www.sheknows.com/parenting/articles/819528/5-parenting-styles-for-a-new-ge.

Mosle, S. (2013). The dicey parent-teacher duet. Retrieved from http://opinionator.blogs.nytimes.com/2013/01/11/the-dicey-parent-teacher-duet/.

Naumberg, C. (2012). What is mindful parenting? Retrieved from http://www.huffingtonpost.com/carla-naumburg/mindful-parenting_b_2198097.html.

The New York Times. (2011a). Calling mom a hippo. Retrieved from http://parenting.blogs.nytimes.com/2011/04/27/calling-mom-a-hippo/.

The New York Times. (2011b). Panda dads and parenting goals. Retrieved from http://parenting.blogs.nytimes.com/2011/03/30/panda-dads-and-parenting-goals/.

Partnership for 21st Century Skills. (2004). *The partnership for 21st century skills-Framework for 21st century learning*. Retrieved November 1, 2011, from http://www.p21.org/.

Pickert, K. (2012). The man who remade motherhood. *Time Magazine*, Monday, May 21.

Rosenfeld, A., and N. Wise. (2001). *The Over-Scheduled Child: Avoiding the Hyper-Parenting Trap*. New York: St. Martin's Griffin.

Scheve, T. (n.d.) What are some of the different parenting styles? Retrieved from http://tlc.howstuffworks.com/family/parenting-styles5.htm.

Sears, Sheri. (2010). Are you a yes-mom or a no-mom. Retrieved from http://heartofthematteronline.com/are-you-a-yes-mom-or-a-no-mom/.

Sedacca, R. (2013). Children parenting their parents: A dangerous consequence of divorce. Retrieved from http://www.huffingtonpost.com/rosalind-sedacca/children-parenting-their-_b_3112321.html.

Skenazy, L. (2009). *Free-Range Kids: How to Raise Safe, Self-Reliant Children (Without Going Nuts with Worry)*. San Francisco: John Wiley & Sons.

Skolnik, D. (2012). Stop being a micromanaging mom, Deborah. *Parenting, 26(2 Mar)*, pp. 76–79.

Solter, A. (1989). *Helping Young Children Flourish*. Shining Star Press.

Sotonoff, J. (2011). What type of parent are you? Parenting styles. *Daily Herald*, 20 Apr: 6.

Spock, B. (1946). *The Common Sense Book of Baby and Child Care*. New York: Duell, Sloan and Pearce.

Strauss, R. (2011). Reflections of a "pussycat dad." *Forward* [New York, N.Y] 04 Mar.

Sze, K. (2013). "Snow plow" parenting becoming new trend. Retrieved from http://abclocal.go.com/kgo/story?section=news/health&id=8994417.

Wade, L. (2010). Parenting style may affect teen drinking. Retrieved from http://thechart.blogs.cnn.com/2010/06/25/parenting-style-may-affect-teen-drinking/.

CPSIA information can be obtained at www.ICGtesting.com
Printed in the USA
BVOW03*1141080614

355475BV00005B/2/P